LIPSTICK SELF-TALK

A RADICAL LITTLE SELF-LOVE BOOK

KRISTEN HELMSTETTER

Green
Butterfly
Press

VI.2

ABOUT THE AUTHOR

In 2018, Kristen Helmstetter sold everything to travel the world with her husband and daughter. She currently splits her time between the United States and a medieval hilltop town in Umbria, Italy.

She writes romance novels under the pen name Brisa Starr.

Listen to *Coffee Self-Talk with Kristen Helmstetter* wherever you listen to podcasts.

You can also find her on Instagram:

 instagram.com/coffeeselftalk

OTHER BOOKS BY KRISTEN HELMSTETTER

Coffee Self-Talk: 5 Minutes a Day to Start Living Your Magical Life

The Coffee Self-Talk Daily Readers (#1 & #2): Bite-Sized Nuggets of Magic to Add to Your Morning Routine

Pillow Self-Talk: 5 Minutes Before Bed to Start Living the Life of Your Dreams

Wine Self-Talk: 15 Minutes to Relax & Tap Into Your Inner Genius

Tea Time Self-Talk: A Little Afternoon Bliss for Living Your Magical Life

The Coffee Self-Talk Guided Journal: Writing Prompts & Inspiration for Living Your Magical Life

The Coffee Self-Talk Starter Pages: A Quick Daily Workbook to Jumpstart Your Coffee Self-Talk

Coffee Self-Talk for Dudes: 5 Minutes a Day to Start Living Your Legendary Life

Coffee Self-Talk for Teen Girls: 5 Minutes a Day for Confidence, Achievement & Lifelong Happiness

COMING SOON

Money Self-Talk

I dedicate this book to you.

May you light your candle in the dark and see your way through,
knowing you need to do this, and loving yourself enough
to bring the sparkle into your life.

Some women fear the fire, some women simply become it.

— R.H. SIN

CONTENTS

INTRODUCTION

Dear Beautiful Reader,

When I look back to the time before I discovered self-love, and when I compare it to my life today, it reminds me of the first time I realized my daughter needed glasses. We were seated in a restaurant, and I looked across the room and saw a picture on the wall with a cool quote on it. I said to Kamea, who was eight years old at the time, "Hey, look at that picture. Cool quote, huh?"

She looked across the room and said, "Where?"

I pointed to the wall and said, "Right over there, the blue picture hanging on the wall."

"Where, Mom?"

"What do you mean 'where?' Right over there!"

"Oh, there's words on that? I can't read it."

I turned to her, my eyes wide. "What do you mean? Stop messing around. Of course you can."

"No, Mom. I can't."

Skip forward a week. We'd been to the eye doctor, and her new pair of glasses arrived in the mail.

She put them on.

Oh my gosh, the look on her face!

In that instant, her world was forever changed. She now sees clearly.

That's how I feel, too, now that I've discovered self-love. My life will never be the same now that I see, so clearly, that the path to living a magical life begins with a foundation of rock-solid self-love. And I can never unsee this. I'd never want to. But, boy-oh-boy, it was quite the journey getting here.

It all started with a tugging in my soul. A feeling, a begging—*a knowing*—that life is meant to be lived with sparkle. Zest. *Magic.* That tugging started some years ago when we were living in Arizona...

But wait. Before I get to that story...

I want to share something cool I've learned along the way. It's your first lesson in self-love. It's about *vulnerability.* Did you know that **allowing yourself to be vulnerable is actually an act of self-love?**

- Being vulnerable means loving yourself enough *to be yourself.*
- It means stepping through life, putting yourself out there because you feel worthy.
- It opens up your spirit, and it stokes the fire in your soul.

Sure, it's scary to be vulnerable, at least the first few times. But then you get used to it, and you become comfortable just throwing yourself out there. Like Theodore Roosevelt's eloquent, famous quote that moves my spirit every time I read it...

"It is not the critic who counts; not the man who points out how the strong man stumbles, or where the doer of deeds could have done them better. The

credit belongs to the man who is actually in the arena, whose face is marred by dust and sweat and blood; who strives valiantly; who errs, who comes short again and again, because there is no effort without error and shortcoming; but who does actually strive to do the deeds; who knows great enthusiasms, the great devotions; who spends himself in a worthy cause; who at the best knows in the end the triumph of high achievement, and who at the worst, if he fails, at least fails while daring greatly, so that his place shall never be with those cold and timid souls who neither know victory nor defeat."

With that in mind, I'm going to share some things about my life in this book. I'm going to be vulnerable and share with you the stories in my heart. Doing this exercises my own self-love muscle. And besides, those stories are the juiciest, right?

Let's start with a glimpse into my past. In the first three decades of my life...

- I spent my share of time on the couch (3 psychologists and 1 psychiatrist).
- I came from a broken home (my parents split when I was very young). Mom raised my brother and me, so I grew up without having my dad in much of my life. During much of that time, my mom sometimes struggled to put food on the table and went through multiple marriages.
- I spent much of my youth feeling a bit lost, and covering it up with pseudo-confidence, pretending I didn't care and that it didn't affect me. But it did.
- As a young girl, I sank to some dark depths. At times, I wanted to harm myself.
- I had stress to the point of causing physical ailments, even back in high school.
- I married someone when my soul was lost at sea, and I saw him as a life raft. I soon learned that the raft had holes in it. That marriage drowned. Divorce.
- I've been under $100,000 of soul-crushing debt, waking up every day in terror, paralyzed by fear.

- I've been laid off jobs. There were times when I had no idea what would happen next or how I would pay my bills.
- I had body image issues. I battled bulimia and orthorexia.
- I've been abused.
- I had a miscarriage.
- Mood swings ruled my days.

I could go on, but the bottom line is, I've had my share of problems.

Why Does This Matter?

Because *I didn't feel worthy.* And this drove me through a life of bad decisions.

I lived most of my life feeling lost. But I usually shrugged it off, figuring everyone's got problems, right? I mean, don't a lot of kids' parents split up? Don't most young women struggle with body image? And besides, things could be worse. I had food, running water, a roof over my head, and I didn't live in a war zone.

By my late twenties, I'd had some career success, and this became how I defined my worthiness. But it would take me much longer to learn that career success was never going to unlock the door to magical living. Because deep down, I still didn't feel worthy.

Skip forward a few years, when I was living in Arizona with my amazing second husband, Greg, and my young daughter. Now I had a career and a great family. I should feel blessed, right? On top of the world? But I didn't. I awoke most mornings feeling lost. I didn't have any good direction or focus. Or exciting purpose.

I didn't have any sparkle.

On paper, my life looked pretty darned good. But you know what? Sadness and lack of self-worth can kill your soul, no matter how good things look on the outside.

On the inside, my soul started tugging at me. Yearning for more. Something wasn't right. But I didn't know what it was.

Then one day, I was reading a book in bed. It was called *The Global Student,* and it gave me an idea. Greg walked into the room, and I sat up straight and looked him in the eye. I said, "Let's sell it all and travel the world."

He looked at me, thought for a moment, and then replied, "Sure." And that was that. We sold almost everything we owned, packed three suitcases, and flew to Denmark on one-way tickets. The plan was to bounce around Europe for a year or two, living inexpensively by housesitting, and then make our way to other parts of the globe.

About a year into our travels, I was in Italy, sitting in a beautiful cafe in an ancient building, sipping espresso, working from my laptop. Again, on paper, we were living well. *La dolce vita, right?*

But as I sat there, a thought hit me like a ton of bricks... *I was not happy.* At least, not as happy as I should've been, given my circumstances. Sure, I had moments of awe and excitement from our adventures. *But I still didn't have any sparkle.* I didn't have ongoing joy. And I realized that, with this life of exotic world travel, all I'd managed to do was distract myself.

After a while, I got tired of it. Tired of fighting with life. Tired of feeling like life was yanking me around by my ponytail. But I had no idea what to do.

So I did what a lot of people do. I tried things like meditation, yoga, eating more omega-3's. I journaled. I exercised more. I got sunshine on my eyelids. I read dozens of personal development books, took courses, and looked to people who seemed to have their shit together. Slowly, I began to transform. Some things worked better than others, while other things were mere Band-Aids.

But all of this wasn't enough...

This dawning eventually brought me to what I've called my "dark night of the soul." That's when I realized that, despite this "great" life we were living, deep down, *I didn't feel like I deserved any of it.* And if I didn't feel worthy, I'd never be happy. No matter how many delicious Spritzes or espressos I drink in a beautiful, ancient corner of Italy. These provided only glimpses of happiness, but then they'd always quickly fade away. I didn't want intermittent pixie dust. I wanted it *all the time.*

I decided to take a magnifying glass to my life, and upon close inspection, I witnessed a constant anxiety bubbling just beneath the surface, not usually causing me to freak out, but also never allowing me to completely relax, or experience the true joy that I now know is the birthright of every human being.

So even though I'd held things together fairly well with my Band-Aid tricks over the years, it wasn't enough to make lasting change. I needed to do something dramatic. I needed to transform into a new person and do something epic, like the Phoenix bird rising from its own ashes. I tore through myself, confronting every fear and decades-old trauma, feeling blind and scared, panicky even, but I kept at it. I yanked out every weed I could find, and it was painful. I mourned the old me who'd held me together for almost forty years. I had become addicted to her calming presence, her noble struggle. But she had to go.

Months passed, and I continued working on myself. One morning—and it's a story I've told many times—I was sitting in my tiny Italian kitchen looking out the window. I was ready to take another step. I had an insight: To become the person I wanted to be, I would need new thoughts. New words. New behaviors. I decided to start that morning. With my coffee.

I pulled out my phone, put it in airplane mode, and instead of doing the things that would reinforce the "old me," like scrolling through mind-numbing social media or jumping into business and emails like a crazed rabbit, I opened the Notes application on my iPhone, and I started typing positive self-talk affirmations. *I am worthy. I am confident. I love myself.* I typed lines about living an amazing life, about loving my body. About my worth. About my dream life with money, happiness, and health.

And something amazing happened.

I felt a sparkle!

I still cry, even now, writing this to you, because on that fateful morning, my soul experienced a tiny spark of life. And in that moment, I knew I was onto something big. My intuition screamed to keep going, knowing there was more waiting for me. There was a pot of gold at the end of this rainbow, if only I'd keep at it.

So I kept doing this little ritual—sipping coffee, saying affirmations—every morning for about three weeks, and every day got brighter and brighter. I was finding myself. Transforming. *Blossoming.*

I finally told my husband that I was doing this little thing every morning I called *"Coffee Self-Talk."* He looked straight at me, eyes twinkling with excitement, and he said, *"That's a book. You need to write it!"*

And that is how my book, *Coffee Self-Talk,* came to be.

When I discovered the truly massive power of my mind using daily self-talk, I found a strength I'd never known. I'd say that self-talk saved me, but actually, *I saved myself, using my self-talk.* And here I am, years later, living what I can only describe as an amazing, magical life. A life I never dreamed I'd be living back in those difficult times.

Getting where I am today took real work. It required showing up, every day, caring for my mind, and loving the heck out of myself. Along the way, I yanked up more weeds that I found lurking here and there, but every step of the process forced me to take a strong look at my behaviors, and my thoughts, and my feelings, and sort them out, putting them in the right, magical place.

I want to tell my story to the world, so people everywhere will think, *"If she did it, so can I."* Because I am not unique. I am not the only person whose life can be turned around using self-talk. I was just a woman, trudging along, trying to be optimistic, but somehow always losing my way. If this process worked for me, it can work for anybody.

Why Lipstick?

In *Coffee Self-Talk: 5 Minutes a Day to Start Living Your Magical Life*, I described how important self-love is for living your magical life. What I didn't realize at the time was that I need to say *a lot* more about that! It turns out, many people are running very low on self-love, self-worth, and self-esteem these days.

I kept hearing variations of the same comment: *"I love the idea of Coffee Self-Talk, but how do I find even 5-minutes to start? I have a two-year old."*

Wow! So many people out there who feel they can't even sit down and have a cup of coffee, even if it might change their whole life. What does that say about the person? It says they're not taking care of themselves. Not making themselves a priority. Not loving themselves. I understand the feeling—I've been there myself—but there's a reason the flight attendant tells you to put on your own oxygen mask first... so you'll be capable of then helping others. Self-care is no different. And too many people aren't taking care of themselves enough to do the very thing that will give them control over their lives.

They're stuck in a *helplessness loop*. They can't get out of the loop, because they feel helpless to take the steps that would get them out of the loop!

This pulled on my heart as I realized some people need something more in their toolbox. A way to jump-start the self-love cycle. Something that doesn't even take five minutes!

Presenting *Lipstick Self-Talk!* A book that's focused exclusively on self-love, with a technique that takes even less time than drinking a cup of coffee. Something you can do in a few seconds, multiple times a day, while you're putting on your lipstick or lip balm. It's that easy!

So this book is for all of you who are not loving yourselves enough, because you're too busy putting other people first: the parents, the people-pleasers, the guilt-ridden. It's for the perfectionists. It's for the people who know there's a better way to live, it's tugging at your soul and whispering to you in the night, but you don't know where to start.

By the time you're done with this book, you'll be standing tall, proud, with your own superhero self-love swirling around you. *Powerful.* Loving yourself like you've never done before. You'll discover how your own self-love makes you a beautiful badass, and helps your loved ones at the same time, because you'll discover a powerful secret about life...

- That, as you honor your own light, you honor the light in others.
- As you take care of yourself first, you end up helping others better.
- You will be better at everything in your life and for everyone, after you love yourself.

In other words, you put on your own freakin' oxygen mask first!

And when you love yourself like you were born to do... your world opens up, you become free. You become resilient, because you build the most amazing foundation of self-love.

It's time for some hot n' sassy, razzle-dazzle, soul-filled stuff. It's time for lighter and brighter days. Flowers and Sunshine. Love and enjoyment. It's time to start you on *your* journey to sparkling self-love and soul-shining self-worth.

Okay. Are you ready to sparkle, smile, and play? Because I am.

Let's do this!

I love you to the moon and back,

Kristen

P.S. A special note if you're someone who needs the following message right now... As I'm typing these words, I'm feeling a pull to you, and I want you to know that I believe in you. Think of me as some strange woman out there who gives a damn about you and your happiness, like we're connected somehow. You are beautiful, and you have wisdom, experiences, and stories to tell. I appreciate the heck out of you.

P.P.S. Do you know those awesome "gifts with purchase" you get at the makeup counter? You buy some makeup and walk away with a little bag full of freebie makeup treasure? Well, with that in mind, at the end of this book, there's a little special gift for you. (It's okay if you want to go look now!)

CHAPTER 1

THE SKINNY ON SELF-TALK

To love oneself is the beginning of a life-long romance.

— OSCAR WILDE

What the Heck Is Self-Talk?

Before I explain what Lipstick Self-Talk is, I will explain what self-talk is in general.

Self-talk is one of the most important things in your life. That's because, when you're doing it wrong, it hurts you. But when you do it right, it makes your life magical. **In other words, your self-talk makes or breaks you.**

What is self-talk? Self-talk is simply the thoughts you think and the words you say, about yourself, the world, and your life.

Every thought that flows through your mind that has to do with you, your accomplishments, your mistakes, your opportunities, your problems, your health, your body, your opinions, your judgments (about yourself and others), where you are in your life right now, the things you want in your life... all of that is self-talk.

So, as you can imagine, your self-talk can be good or bad, because what you think about yourself, the world, or life can be good or bad. In this book, you are going to learn exactly what to say with your self-talk.

But before we get to that, we must begin with one central idea. And that is, the way to live your best life comes from loving yourself. Loving yourself comes directly from having good self-talk. *Really good* self-talk. Good words, good thoughts, good feelings. Your health, your relationships, your career, your prosperity, your life... *everything* is tied to the simple thoughts you think about yourself, both consciously and unconsciously. How you feel about yourself is the driving force behind whether you have a good day, a so-so day, or a crappy day. They are the reason you believe certain things and behave in certain ways. It's the reason you're either manifesting a magical life or a stressed-out life. It all starts with your self-talk.

This book is designed to help you change your self-talk so it's *alllll good*.

Why It Matters: Because it's in changing our self-talk that we find our way to loving ourselves.

So, in order to have a magical life, you have to love yourself, because if you don't love yourself, deep down, you won't think you're worthy of having the life of your dreams, and you'll sabotage your progress, or simply quit.

Self-Talk and Chocolate Cake

Let's think of the self-talk process like baking a chocolate cake. If you want to make a chocolate cake, you start with a chocolate cake recipe. Does your recipe for chocolate cake include ground beef? No. Are you going to mix in some grass clippings? No. Are you going to put pasta in it? No. What are you going to put into it? You're going to put in *chocolate cake ingredients*: You know, flour, chocolate, eggs, sugar, butter, etc.

The results you get come from the ingredients you put in.

The same thing happens with your life. If you want a happy life, or success at work, or a great romance, then you must start with the right ingredients: the right self-talk. This good, positive self-talk brings you the good, positive results you deserve.

Let's Try Some Self-Talk

Say the following out loud, and say it with gusto, like you really mean it:

"I Love Me!"

How was it? Was it easy? Was it weird? Was it difficult? Was it so hard to say that you didn't even actually do it? If you had a hard time saying it, don't worry. Have faith. With the help of this book, your subconscious mind will get reprogrammed to the point that you love thinking about loving yourself in a beautiful, kind, generous way.

Yes, Self-Talk Can Be Totally Weird at First!

When you first start doing positive self-talk, and you start telling yourself how much you love yourself, it can seem very weird. Even downright silly. It can be a bit jarring and feel foreign, but you keep at it. You keep doing the self-talk every day, and then, one day, you get used to it. It just stops feeling weird.

And then?

- It shifts to being magical.
- You love it.
- You want more of it.

This powerful way of speaking becomes your new, radical, star-bright default. Repetition and frequency are the key, though. You keep showing up for it.

You go about your life, moving through your day. You just keep repeating your favorite affirmations. And when you're not speaking, you're thinking them. Ten, twenty, or even 100 times in any day. Believe me, it *will* take root. And, darling, when it does, it's awesome. You become a new person.

There might be a day now and then when you get knocked off your unicorn, but because sparkling self-talk is your new habit, you return to it, like you're on autopilot. And this puts you back on track.

But Wait, Is Self-Talk Lying to Myself?

If I tell myself I love myself, when I don't love myself, am I lying? When I say I feel beautiful, even though I don't, is this lying? Or when I say I'm happy, even though I'm feeling down, is this not lying?

No, positive self-talk is not lying. Lying is about deception. You're not deceiving anybody. No, this is *reprogramming*. In fact, it's the exact opposite of lying, in that you are reprogramming your brain with a new *truth*. A blueprint. *Instructions* about how to think, and what to believe. Self-talk is telling our brains how we are *meant* to be, how we should've been for our whole lives, but somewhere along the way, we took a wrong turn. And with practice, you'll see that loving yourself is easy, fluid, and addictive. For now, good ol' "fake it till you make it" does wonders. It really works.

So keep repeating your positive self-talk. Even if you don't believe all of your affirmations just yet, you will soon. Repetition is your very, very best friend. The more you say your positive self-talk, the quicker you train your brain and start to believe what you're saying.

- Once you believe in yourself, everything else just falls into place, as though by magic.

- Belief is what fuels your drive, your decisions, your efforts, and your success.

Is Loving Myself All Ego?

At first, I wondered if constantly telling myself "I love me" would give me a bigfoot-sized ego (it was especially bizarre saying these words to myself in the mirror). But don't worry, an out-of-control ego is not what happens. Outsized egos come from insecurity, not security. When you love yourself, you feel safe, and your ego feels safe, meaning it doesn't get all crazy and out of control. The kind of self-love I write about comes from your heart, from a place of kindness, appreciation, and generosity. That's the farthest thing in the world from having a huge ego.

When you love yourself, you stop judging yourself so harshly, and this is a beautiful thing because you naturally stop judging others, too. You no longer seek to validate yourself by comparing yourself or feeling superior to others. Loving yourself actually infuses compassion, for yourself *and others*, and that's world-changing. If more people simply loved themselves, we would have so much more compassion in the world, not selfish, ego-driven behavior.

Loving yourself isn't vanity; it's sanity.

— KATRINA MAYER

How Long Does This Take to Work?

Some people feel a little something happening the first time they say positive self-talk. For others, it might take a few weeks to start noticing a change in how they feel. In general, the time it takes depends on how often you show up to your life and do your self-talk ritual.

Sometimes your transformation starts in the background, and you don't notice it immediately, but you sense something is happening. Or you might see little examples now and then, which cause you to sit up. And even though you want some big wins right now—*don't we all wish we could throw a penny in the fountain, make a wish, and have it appear right away?*—it doesn't always work that way. Some of these things take time. So you keep believing and keep showing up each day, doing your Lipstick Self-Talk, and keep your mind focused on the right words. You *will* find your epic self-love.

You're Here, Now

You're reading this book because you want to make a change. You want a better life. And now it's time to move forward. It's time to redefine who you are and what you stand for.

You're here because something is missing from your day. Missing from your life. It's you. *You're* what's missing! And we're here to find you. Your most authentic, beautiful, *amazing you*. Your new life starts this very second. It's time to fall madly in love with yourself!

You're about to turn up the magic in your life.

Say it with me:

I choose to be worthy.

I decide I am worthy.

I choose what I get to believe in.

I decide what I believe in.

I am worthy of this, I believe in me, and my beautiful life is right here for me.

I am taking action.

Why Don't More People Love Themselves?

Most of us never learned how to properly love ourselves. We didn't know that we are actually, truly, *supposed to love ourselves, first*. If we had been born with a user's guide, it would have clearly stated in Chapter 1: *Love Yourself Big Time.*

We didn't understand that self-love is the golden key to happiness, a happiness that no money can buy. Loving yourself is medicine for your soul. It's freedom. It's healing. It's resilience and courage in the face of anything.

When we were growing up, our parents played a crucial role in helping us understand love, and whatever they taught us is based largely on how they love themselves, which was taught to them by their parents. I have family members who don't love themselves, and as a result, they didn't teach me to love myself to the fullest. My parents divorced when I was very young, and my dad didn't do a great job of showing love. But he also didn't love himself very much, and I know where he got that—from *his* parents. So, you see? It trickles down through the generations, until someone breaks the pattern.

It ran in the family until it ran into me.

— BRIAN FULLER

Why This Matters: Where you are right now, mentally and emotionally, is based on old wiring in your brain. Even from way back in your childhood, like it was for me. If you're not shining like a bright star, it's not your fault. Even among kids with great childhoods, most were still never taught about their hidden superpower: *words*. Most of us weren't taught about the critical ingredient to a magical life: self-love.

Grab Your Magnifying Glass and Explore

If you were to peer deep inside your brain at this wiring, you'd see patterns and behaviors that were programmed when you were a child. When I took a closer look at my programming, I was shocked at the crusty-ass wiring in my head. Wiring that I was still firing constantly, *unknowingly*. But there it was. My brain was full of poor, body image bullshit (I know exactly where it came from, and it's no wonder I had eating disorders). I also embraced "put others first" behaviors from watching my mom do that with me. (She thought she was doing the right thing by always putting me first.) I filled my head with what others deemed was being a "good" mother, even though these things were wearing me down. It's no wonder I had such a rough go with my first few years as a mom.

There's a name for this, where we do as we see others do. It's called *mirroring*. We even have special neurons in our brains for this process called *mirror neurons*.

This means that, when we see other people doing something, our brains fire and wire thoughts and behaviors that mirror what we see. The more we see something, the stronger the pattern gets wired in our brain. This is beneficial when your brain mirrors good things. Over generations, it helped people survive and adapt because it allows us to learn what is good and safe, or bad and dangerous. But mimicking our parents is just a starting point for learning how to survive and thrive. Once we're old enough to take responsibility for ourselves, it's better to be mindful of where we get our influences and take control of what's being programmed into our brains. And we do this using self-talk.

Take a Look

If you look closely at your habits and the things that bring you joy, you can trace much of it back to your youth. If you grew up with a parent who responded poorly to stress, then there's a good chance you'll have that wiring in your brain, too. If you grew up with a parent who didn't respect themselves or love themselves, that way of life gets fired and wired in your brain, and it can program you with similar negative behaviors. It's interesting to look back and take stock of what you've "learned"—to see if it serves the best you, today.

So you didn't create your current level of self-love or self-worth alone. There were influences from family, and friends, and partners, and life experiences. But now you know better, and guess what? You have control over this! You have the power to change the old wiring in your mind. You are the master conductor of your life.

If you look back and see things you don't like, don't worry. Don't punish yourself. Don't blame others. The past is behind you. All that matters is what you do now. You can change tomorrow by changing your today. And that's what we're going to do in the next chapter.

In today already walks tomorrow.

— SAMUEL TAYLOR COLERIDGE

Exercise

Earlier in this chapter, I described how the recipe for chocolate cake has things like flour, sugar, chocolate, and so on. If you were going to write down the recipe for the new, self-loving you, what ingredients would you include? Would you include ingredients like compassion, serenity, relaxation, contemplation? Or perhaps focus, drive, determination, and perseverance? Write down as many ingredients for the new you as you like.

CHAPTER 2

WHAT IS LIPSTICK SELF-TALK?

Your destiny is determined by your decisions. Your decisions are determined by your thinking. Change your thinking, change your destiny.

— BRIAN TRACY

- Lipstick Self-Talk is a 60-second self-care ritual that creates a deep well of self-love to help you live your best life ever.
- The ritual is simple: You put on your lipstick (or lip balm) and repeat powerful lines of self-talk while you do it. (From here on out, I'll usually just refer to lipstick. If you're more into lip balm, that works 100%.)
- This process takes advantage of repetition, mirror magic, and your self-talk. (More on mirror magic below.)

If you're a reader of my books, then you know I've found many ways to add self-talk to my life that go beyond just my morning coffee ritual (Coffee Self-Talk). I also do it in the afternoon with tea, I do it at night with my pillow, and I sometimes do it with a glass of wine.

One day, I realized there was another perfect moment for more juicy self-talk... when I was putting on my lipstick. And it became one of the most powerful times to do self-talk, for four reasons:

1. Using a mirror is a HUGE way to amp up the magic!
2. Applying lipstick is an affirmative, self-care ritual in itself... a mini-dose of *girl power*. Attaching words to this ritual leverages that power.
3. It's so fast and easy, it's essentially effortless.
4. Unlike morning coffee, you can do it multiple times a day.

Traditional self-talk instructions make no mention of putting on lipstick. But by anchoring the process to your make-up routine, you anchor thoughts and words that change your life. Your self-talk comes across your lipsticked lips, and this connection creates more meaning. You see yourself in the mirror, and more importantly, you acknowledge yourself by doing this.

Boost Your Mood Multiple Times a Day

My success comes from showing up every day to love myself. In many instances, many times a day. Lipstick is just another way I take advantage of a momentary break in my day to step into my most self-loving mental state. Because we put on our lipstick multiple times a day, we get these little infusions of mood-boosting brilliance every time. With Lipstick Self-Talk, you're summoning, on demand, your most empowered mental state every time you put on your lipstick! When you combine the two, lipstick and self-talk, you link them together in your brain with tremendous impact.

Color your lips, and color your mind!

A typical woman might swipe on her lipstick anywhere from five to ten times a day. Think about that... **this creates multiple magical**

opportunities to focus your lips on something that will change your life.

Why This Is So Special

- When you ritualize a behavior, you give it special meaning.
- This meaning gives it more importance, which makes you take it more seriously.
- The more ceremonial you make your rituals, the more power they have. And because rituals are repeated, they become partly automated, which is the key to establishing something as a habit.

All of these help to reprogram your brain and change your *belief* in yourself. And self-belief is one of the most important ingredients to your success. If you don't believe something is possible, you won't even attempt it. But when you do believe that something is not only possible—but *probable*—then *look out, world!*

Another ingredient of success is plain old perseverance, just sticking with something long enough for it to work. Whether it's exercise, a diet, a financial plan, or career advancement, persistence makes all the difference. It trains your brain. It moves you along. It keeps you going through the rough spots.

Change Your Life with Lipstick! 💄💋

When you link self-talk to a part of your daily routine that you're very unlikely to skip, then you actually do it almost every day. Just imagine the long-term, compounding benefits to your well-being and success. This is called "habit stacking," which I discussed in *Coffee Self-Talk*, where I linked self-talk to my morning habit of drinking coffee. With Lipstick Self-Talk, we'll be linking self-talk with the habit of putting on your lipstick.

The other intriguing bit is that Lipstick Self-Talk is a *multi-sensory modality*. In other words, it's more than words. Using multiple senses activates more parts of your brain, which makes stronger connections as you rewire yourself with great, new, positive thoughts.

- I'm linking my ritualized self-talk to the act of swiping a color across my lips (*feeling* the lipstick's cream or tack or slipperiness, and *seeing* it on my lips).
- Whenever possible, I'm saying the words out loud (*hearing* it), and that means I connect the words I say to the *feel* of putting on the lipstick, and then *seeing* it on me in the mirror.
- Some lipsticks have a particular smell. You can anchor that too, so you get to the point where just smelling your lipstick reminds you of your self-talk.
- Basically, the more senses you involve when doing your self-talk, the more energy you can put into getting results faster.

And let's just face it... lipstick is fun!

Mirror Magic

But there's another *super* important part as to why Lipstick Self-Talk is *such a powerful ritual*. That's because of the role the mirror plays in it.

Doing self-talk in front of the mirror is not new, though it will certainly be new to some people. Have you ever had a conversation with yourself in the mirror? Maybe you've practiced what you'd say to someone on a date, or you rehearsed a speech you were about to give. People have been using mirrors to practice forever.

I first read about doing self-talk in front of a mirror from author Louise Hay in my thirties, but people have been doing it much longer. In the 1940s, Claude Bristol wrote about people like Winston Churchill and Woodrow Wilson practicing important speeches in the mirror first, before addressing large crowds of people. He also writes

about organizations in the 1930s using mirrors that were strategically placed around the office with slogans (ahem, *self-talk*) written on them in soap, so that it would be easy to change the slogans every day. The salespeople would see these throughout the day and build up their self-confidence. These organizations did very well, even during the Great Depression.

The mirror shows a reflection of you. And what you say to yourself in the mirror *becomes your power*. Most people look in the mirror and find flaws... I know I used to. But that all changed when I became strategic with my self-talk, and it *really* changed when I started doing it in front of the mirror. If you want to program your subconscious in a profound way, then do Lipstick Self-Talk!

When I use a mirror and say my affirmations—while looking into my own eyes—something magical stirs inside of me. I watch my lips move, I hear my words, I feel my face and body come to life. I stand taller... there's an almost mystical energy that comes about, like I'm creating my destiny with a spell! Don't laugh—well, okay, go ahead and giggle—but it's true, I am in awe of how I feel when I look at myself in the mirror and really *see myself*, and then say words of love and confidence to myself. It's epic.

Yes, it seemed weird at first. And even a bit disingenuous (and, um, silly) to talk to myself in the mirror. But it was fascinating, too. And once you get past any awkwardness (and you will, I *promise*), you feel like a star. That moment of looking into your own eyes is powerful, because using a mirror drives your beliefs deeper into you. It packs a wallop on your subconscious and grabs your attention like nothing else, and your self-love soars because you start to really recognize yourself.

It's like giving your words a Disney FastPass from your brain to your heart!

In addition to the repetition, by doing your self-talk in front of the mirror, *you will* get to belief faster, because you are in front of your-

self, and there's nowhere to hide. It's like an intervention with yourself. You are you, and you are right there.

So speak your positive self-talk, even if your voice shakes, even if your mind shakes, even if your heart shakes. Keep doing it. Keep showing up, because you are worthy, and amazing, and so very, very awesome.

How to Do Lipstick Self-Talk!

Take this book and stand in front of the mirror, tall, proud, honored to be with yourself, shoulders back... and look into your own eyes. Take a deep breath, and feel your power filling your body. Your strength. You will see it reflected in your eyes, and the true you is revealed. And you are beautiful, inside and out. Know that. *Please* know that! *Feel* that.

- Select a script from this book (you can start with the one below, and then move on to the scripts included at the end of the other chapters).
- Pick up your lipstick, and swipe some on.
- Read through the script you chose, out loud, and take a second to *really* look at yourself between each line. Extra credit if you blow yourself a kiss, give yourself a wink or a nod, or simply stare into your eyes for an extra-long, hot second. These are all just additional ways of acknowledging yourself.
- Do this ritual every time you put on your lipstick or lip balm throughout the day, whether it's sitting at your vanity, standing in front of the bathroom mirror at work, looking at your reflection in the restroom at your local coffee shop, getting dressed at the gym after a workout, or sitting in your parked car looking into the rearview mirror.
- Smile at yourself. Revel in the twinkle of your eyes that you are on *the most important journey of your life.*

Alrighty, let's get started with your very first Lipstick Self-Talk script. Grab your lipstick and go to a mirror. You know what to do...

Lipstick Self-Talk

I am worthy of living the most amazing life.

I am beautiful, confident, and full of wonder.

I choose great words so that I can have a great life!

I am overflowing with love.

All is good. So very, very beautifully good.

CHAPTER 3

RADICAL SELF-R.E.S.P.E.C.T.

What you think of yourself, that is what determines your fate.

— Henry David Thoreau

My journey into a life of happiness was like peeling an onion. Every time I evolved or transformed, and made my life better, I found more things to transform. Another layer to peel. It was as though I started with the big things first, and once those were taken care of, I found more things to learn and change.

When I first began this journey, strangely, I never gave much thought to self-respect. The idea just didn't cross my mind. But as I dug deeper into making my life magical, I came to see how vital it is to well-being, self-love, and magical living.

Why do I call it "radical" self-respect? Because sometimes we need to shake things up. Sometimes we need to make something really big and profound in order to pay attention to it. Sometimes we need to give ourselves permission to take something on, in a big way, because it's so important to us. As such, radical self-respect is a big concept in this book. It's time to blow the roof off and give yourself the respect you deserve!

Self-Respect for Better Decisions and Better Living

When you have self-love, you have self-respect. And when you have this, you make better decisions, because you lose the subconscious desire to hold yourself back. And when you have self-respect, you also make those decisions faster and easier. You don't waffle. You just *know*.

When we have self-respect, we walk away from things that don't serve our higher needs. When we have self-respect, we smile inwardly to ourselves, no matter what others might say or do. Their opinions cease to matter. Self-respect is an invisible shield of strength; it's like our bones get stronger, and our blood gets *shimmerier*.

Self-respect is all of these things to me.

Why Self-Respect Feels So Good

Have you ever heard of *serotonin*? The word comes up a lot in the context of antidepressants. Serotonin is a neurochemical that gets secreted in your brain when you do certain things, and it changes your mood, makes you feel great. When serotonin sparkles inside your brain, it feels *really* good. It helps you feel calm. It makes you feel strong, capable, and confident.

What behaviors trigger this cascade of good serotonin feelings? It happens when you gain a position of strength. When you assert yourself. Your brain rewards you with this delightful feeling when you behave confidently from your position of *belief in yourself*. And this happens whenever you respect yourself. For example, if you are in a work meeting, and you respect yourself and your ideas, you're much more likely to assert yourself in the meeting. And when you do, it feels good. It's a take-charge attitude, and it gives you peace of mind.

Another great way to enjoy more bursts of serotonin is to take steps and make progress toward your goals. So take pride in your efforts. Take pride in your self-love. And take pride with your self-respect. Set goals that motivate you to take action, and break them down into small, easy, baby steps. With each step you take, or each item you cross off your to-do list, you'll feel pride and self-respect, and you'll give yourself a nice *drip drip drip* of delicious serotonin.

You can even use this technique to make yourself feel great when doing things you don't even like doing. For example, when it's time to do my taxes, I break up the process into really small, almost comical, steps. For example, on day one, I get out my yellow legal pad. That's it! On day two, I print out my credit card statements. That's it. And from there, I continue doing my taxes in tiny, easily accomplished steps, feeling good each time I check an item off the list.

Or when it's time to vacuum, I get out the vacuum early in the day and put it in the middle of the room—no lie! First step completed! It's still a step, and I feel good about it. And I'm much more likely to vacuum if it's out. Silly, right? Who cares? And again, I take pride in this first tiny step, because I made progress toward my goal. Sounds crazy, but it really works.

Once you complete one step toward a goal, then you simply set another stepping-stone goal. And then another, and another, and as you accomplish your goals, your self-respect grows and blossoms, because you feel proud for taking action and getting things done. And when you take pride in your steps, you build new neural pathways for experiencing that juicy serotonin-feeling, and you build self-respect, which builds your foundation of self-love.

Serotonin and Social Media: A Dangerous Mix

As many of my readers know, I'm not a huge fan of social media. Recognition from others can boost your feel-good serotonin levels and cause you to feel pleasure in the short term, but that's part of the problem... it's only temporary. It leaves you wanting more and more recognition, likes, and approval. This is one reason social media is so addictive for some people. Even worse, when you compare yourself to others—*and if you're in a position to feel like you are doing "well" in comparison to others, or if somebody else recognizes your efforts*—then you feel good.

This can be very damaging. It can create a constant need for validation *from other people*. You can become addicted to such praise, addicted to it as a source of feel-good serotonin. The need to compare ourselves to others is a natural human instinct, as social status has been linked to survival since our hunter-gatherer days. We not only seek status, but when we get it, we *like how it feels*, reinforcing our desire for more. This can become a vicious, addictive feedback loop, and it can throw you into a funk when the recognition stops.

I do seek the good feelings of serotonin, but frankly, I choose to feel pride because of my own standards, not because I compare them to someone else. I want to be addicted to my own results by comparing them to my past results and witnessing my own growth.

The other risk from spending too much time on social media comes when you compare yourself to others, and you feel like you're falling behind in life. This kind of comparing can make you feel bad. But what you must understand is that your adventure is different than everyone else's, and it's leading you to a destination that is uniquely yours. There is no need to compare yourself to others. Again, compare yourself to yourself.

Find your growth by asking yourself, "How am I doing now, as compared to last week, or last month, or last year? And how can I improve that (if it needs to be improved)?"

THE GOOD NEWS: Research shows that, the happier you get with yourself and your life, the less you'll bother with comparing yourself to others. That was my experience, too. I had to first get happier and boost my own self-esteem and self-love before engaging more healthily on social media. I had to get my brain squirting serotonin from my own growth without comparing it to others.

That said, there isn't anything wrong with letting other people *inspire* you to grow and become healthier, wealthier, stronger, happier, etc. You *can* use comparison to push yourself in a positive way, so long as you've got a healthy mindset, with plenty of self-love.

The trap is when...

a) You don't have a healthy mindset, and so when you see other people doing well, it bothers you.

b) You feel pride knowing you're doing better than other people.

Neither of these scenarios are good for you. They both chip away at your self-esteem, so be careful. Feeling good about doing better than others is the sign of a frightened ego defending itself. A well-balanced individual wants to see everyone happy and successful!

Lastly, social media tempts us with the allure of *vanity metrics*—hard numbers... statistics about how well we're doing socially. But there's no way around the fact that we love metrics, and social media sites take full advantage of this. According to an article by Michael Simmons, "The mind loves metrics, especially public metrics. This is why social media platforms can so effectively train us to maximize our followers, Likes, and comments. When these vanity metrics increase, we feel like we're making progress and doing important work."

The secret trick to feeling good from the serotonin boost is to trigger it without using social media or getting stuck in a loop of "comparisonitis." And one of the ways to do this is through boosting your own self-respect!

- Compare yourself *to your former self* as you grow. Track your progress, and reward yourself for small, steady, incremental progress.

- Set a few goals, and notice how good it feels to set them. As you make progress, it feels good because of how it impacts *your* life, not to keep up with the Jones's.
- Track your own efforts, and see how amazing you feel as you make progress.

The great thing is that, when you have self-respect, you'll naturally feel like you're doing well in the world—your own, private world.

Self-Respect Means Putting On Your Big Girl Pants

One thing I learned through my journey was that self-respect must start with me. I had to take responsibility for my own actions. In other words, I had to take responsibility for my own self-respect, which came from my self-love.

When you blame things like culture, or your parents, or other people, you lose your power. You have to take responsibility to look for the silver linings in life. You have to take responsibility and show up to yourself every day and say nice things. *You* have to be the power that drives and controls your own mindset.

Does this seem obvious? It may be obvious to some people, but it's not to everyone... many people are quick to blame anyone but themselves for their situation. Right or wrong, blaming others takes our power away from us. The power to fix it. And even for those of us who are willing to take full responsibility for our lives, we sometimes need a swift little kick in the tushy as a reminder that it is up to us—*at all times*.

Have you ever gone along with something, maybe something with your friends, coworkers, your partner, or a family member, and then later you wished you hadn't? That bad feeling you experience after is what it feels like to lack self-respect. That feeling of, *Why did I do that? I knew better.*

In the pressure of a doctor's office setting, I once consented to a minor medical procedure that, in hindsight, I regret. I wish I had taken the time to research it and make a more informed decision. I don't really believe in living with regret though, so instead, I look at this experience as a lesson. And that lesson is that I'm responsible for my actions. Not the doctor. Not my friends or family members. Me.

Have you ever gone along with something, and then later blamed the other person?

It's so easy to blame others, or the culture in general, as *"just the way it is."* But that's how you lose your own power!

Or how about blaming other things, like the economy, or the weather?

Why didn't you go out for a jog?

Because it was raining.

Rain? No! That is an excuse. People in Seattle jog all the time. When you take the easy or lazy way, or make excuses, you don't feel like you have much self-respect. But flip it around, and imagine you did go run, even though it's raining, and guess what... you feel like a badass! Your self-respect goes *boom!*

This is just one example, but there are so many little instances like this, where you could take the easy road, or give up on something, and that's no recipe for radical self-respect. Start making better choices. Start doing the hard stuff. Start getting your butt out there. It will change your mindset. It will make you feel stronger. It will create a deep self-respect that changes your life. All this, just for running in the rain. :) When you take responsibility and make better choices, no matter how small, you boost your self-respect.

Self-respect is also about honoring your commitments. To yourself and others. Do what you say you'll do. If you make a promise or resolution to learn some Spanish this year, then start doing it. Honor that commitment to yourself, and you'll gain your own respect. You'll feel the difference, every time you study the language, or whatever it is you set out to do. Each step will feel good, and you'll take pride in doing it.

Or if you decide to work out three days a week, then honor that commitment! Do it. Because here's the thing... when you *don't* do it, not only do you *not* get the self-respect boost, but it also goes in the opposite direction. You actually *lose* self-respect, because you know you're not doing what you said you would.

But when you set an intention or a goal, and you actually take the steps, it puts you in a new way of living. You power up your passion and confidence, and these add fuel to your self-love tank. So be disciplined, and honor your commitments. The ones you make to yourself, and the ones you make to others. You *will* feel amazing as a result. I triple-sparkle promise!

I am one of a kind. Extraordinary. A woman with a destiny.

— Victoria Moran

Respect Your Dreams and Abilities

Last but not least, you must respect your *dreams*.

I know so many people who say they wanted to do so many things, but never did, and they have less respect for themselves because they didn't even try. That's not to say you must always succeed, but you want to at least try! That alone gives you the self-respect boost. It's okay if things go a different direction, or something else comes about, but never give up on yourself, and you'll find massive amounts of self-love. And it's always a great time to start, whatever your age.

There is *no excuse* to not go after a dream. It can be a dream for more education, or a healthier body, or starting a new business, or finding the love of your life. We live in a time when it's easier than ever to make our dreams come true.

The Top Chef Episode That Made Me Cry

While I was writing this book, an episode of Top Chef came on, honoring the bold, courageous, and strong women of the past, during a time when they were seen as less than equal by many. It was *Top Chef: Houston*, and the episode was titled, *Texas Trailblaze-hers*. The contestants would create dishes inspired by trailblazing women in Texas history:

- Former Texas governor Ann Richards
- Multi-sport athlete "Babe" Didrikson Zaharias
- Barbara Jordan, the first black woman elected to the U.S. House of Representatives
- Aviator Bessie Coleman
- Singer Selena

I was moved to tears watching this episode. And as I lay in bed later that night, thinking about those women, imagining all the women who lay in their beds before me, like in the 1950s, '40s, '30s and before, I felt infinitely grateful for everything they did *in those much tougher times* to pave the road to make things easier for me. Things they did for me, for you, for our daughters, for our daughters' daughters.

They respected themselves, and that's what pushed them to keep going, and fighting to make the world a better place. They dared to dream, and dared to take action, so we would have the freedoms and ease we have today, *to go after our own dreams and destinies*. To reinvent ourselves at any time! And, for crying out loud, look at what they accomplished, despite the landscape they lived in. Their circumstances didn't stop them, so you definitely aren't going to let today's relatively cushy circumstances stop you. Don't waste everything they've done for us.

Respect these strong women. Respect yourself.

Respect your dreams.

Be your own *SHERO*, and go for it!

Many of these women are no longer with us, but their spirits remain, and they're here beside us, cheering us on. I feel them any time I want, by imagining their spirit right next to me, in fact, right now, as I type these words. They're whispering in my ear... *keep going!*

It's our duty, as women, to honor their efforts and to blaze more trails for the girls and women after us... so *go for it*. Honor your dreams and skills, respect yourself, and go kick some ass.

> *Repeat after me: There can never be too much sky. There can never be too many dreams. There can never be too much coffee. There can never be too many stars. There can never be too much for me.*
>
> — AMANDA LOVELACE

Lipstick Self-Talk

I am my own Shero.

I am worthy of my dreams.

I am disciplined and show up to my life.

I honor my commitments.

I respect myself. Hell yeah, I respect myself.

Exercise

Write about a dream you have, big or small. Whether it's to run a 5K or go back to school. Write why you love this dream, and write one thing you can do to take a step toward it.

CHAPTER 4

AS YOU ARE NOW

To fall in love with yourself is the first secret to happiness.

— Robert Morely

The Perfect Place to Start Right Now: As. You. Are.

Stand in your own fresh, raw power. There is no waiting to do this. Do not wait until you are perfect to love yourself. What is perfection anyway? We are always changing, and there will always be something, some excuse you can come up with. Tomorrow never comes; there is only today. There is no "I'll love myself when..."

For example:

- Don't wait to love yourself when you lose 50 pounds (or 10, or any weight), because loving yourself first is essential for losing the weight.
- Don't wait to love yourself until after you accomplish more, or have more success, because the success will come more effortlessly *after* your self-love starts.

When we really love ourselves, exactly the way we are today, in the moment, right now, everything begins to flow more easily. You'll see little miracles happening everywhere. You attract more goodness and more abundance. Your health, well-being, and energy improve from reduced stress and anxiety. All from just loving yourself the way you are, today.

In the weight-loss example above, when you love yourself now, any weight you want to lose can start to come off you now, "released" by your subconscious. When you feel worthy, you have confidence and speak up for yourself. You can ask for that new job offer, that raise you desire and deserve. Because it's so simple... you feel worthy of it. You're confident. You take more chances. You experiment more.

When you love yourself, today, you'll immediately attract more opportunities and better relationships tomorrow. You smile at a stranger you're attracted to. You connect to others with the bright light that emanates from within you.

But you have to love yourself now. That's where it all begins. And that's what this book teaches you how to do. Trust me, it works.

I will dare to just do what I do. Be just what I am.

— *Beverly Williams*

Challenges Come. That's Fine. It's Called "Life."

The secret is loving ourselves *through* life's challenges. Self-love is the metaphorical bulletproof vest. It's Violet's purple force shield from Disney's movie, *The Incredibles*. When you love yourself, most things just bounce off you. You're able to bob-n-weave. You have the strength to get up again, and again, and again, and keep going.

It's your source of magic. It's your new superpower.

When you don't love yourself, another's harsh criticism can be a slippery slope into crippling self-doubt. But when you love yourself, something amazing happens—you simply don't care about other peoples' opinions as much. You feel protected. You *are* protected. And it's easier to keep an open mind, to glean any feedback that might help you improve.

It's a funny experience when something happens that would have previously knocked you around, but now you find that you no longer have a knee-jerk stressful reaction to it. It's now easy to just shrug things off. What used to cause big waves in your life will be only ripples, and you'll marvel and think, *Wow... this used to bother me?*

This newfound equanimity applies to things both big and small. As for the small, I remember when something as trivial as accidentally breaking a dish, or misplacing my car keys, would send me into a fit, berating myself as though it was the end of the world. Now? I might reflexively cuss the moment I hear the glass crashing on the ground, but two seconds later, I'm reaching for the dustpan and mentally past it, refocused on whatever I was thinking about before. There really is wisdom in that old expression, "crying over spilled milk." Or the more contemporary version, "Don't sweat the small stuff... and it's all small stuff."

As for the big things, imagine, for example, you learn that you have to pick up and move to another city (or state, or even another country). Such an event could easily turn someone's life upside-down. But not when you're protected by your self-love force field! If the cross-country move truly is inevitable (meaning you're past the point of making a decision, and now you're on to making plans), you'll feel only a ripple, if anything at all.

Or! If it's a big wave, no problem... you just grab your surfboard and surf that wave, baby, having fun and being excited about the opportunities, because you're unstoppable with self-love.

Balls-to-the-Wall, Crazy Self-Love

Let's get something straight up front. When I talk about loving your-self, I'm talking about a full on, balls-to-the-wall, crazy love affair with yourself. Not only does it transform who you are, it also becomes a shining example for other people to copy. When you shine your own light with dazzling intensity, its brightness helps light the path for others, who then begin to shine in *their* own light.

With all this love and worthiness also comes a sense of *wholeness*. Feeling complete. When you love yourself, you begin to heal from the inside out. Even physical aches and pains can start to go away, or at least, bother you less. Does self-love make everything in your life perfect? No, but it *feels* more perfect, and you experience a default state of starry confidence and powerful self-worth.

Because, you see, the trick isn't always about changing everything external. It's about digging inside to change the thoughts and patterns in your brain, so you not only *see* a better external reality, but you also bring better things into your life.

From fitness, to food, to relationships, to spending money, to invest-ing, to goals, to making wiser decisions, to coming up with strategies for creating your dream life... you will manifest your dreams faster, if you love yourself first. *It's the foundation of everything.* When you love yourself, everything else you do blossoms, like dumping a giant bucket of pixie dust all over your efforts.

The Wind Beneath Your Wings

Going forward, when you think of self-love, I want you to imagine a beautiful, glorious, colorful bird. When that bird takes off, she's vigor-ously flapping her wings. She's putting in effort, just like you're putting in the effort by showing up multiple times a day to do your Lipstick Self-Talk. And then, very soon, the bird gets to a point where she soars, and the wind beneath her wings allows her to glide with ease, and she catches the currents that lift her ever higher. And that's the reward! Your own self-loving wind carries you!

And just like a bird occasionally flaps her wings to shift direction or climb higher, you continue to show up and do your Lipstick Self-Talk. And then, you get to the point again where you spread your wings, and you soar through life.

Every woman has the right to become herself.

— ANI DIFRANCO

Lipstick Self-Talk

I'm a star, and I'm taking my self-love very far.

I am in the right place, at the right time, for my self-love.

It's a great day for living.

I am free to be me.

I deserve to glitter, sparkle, and shine.

Exercise

The journey to self-love is about finding your true essence. So what is that? Where is the spot in your heart where you feel your highest vibe? What's going on around you when you feel it? When you find it, it feels easy and relaxed. It feels like home.

Close your eyes, and discover it for yourself. Not what your parents want. Not what your friends expect. Not what the world demands. *But you... what do you want? What* do you want to do? *Who* do you want to be? Is it somewhere on the center stage of life? Is it behind the scenes, relaxed, chillin' out in blue jeans? Be still, and take a few minutes right now and try out some different ideas, experiment, play around with it, and see what vision gives you the most peace, the most excitement. In other words, what feels like *home* to you?

CHAPTER 5

STOPPING NEGATIVE SELF-TALK

Love yourself first, and everything else falls into line. You really have to love yourself to get anything done in this world.

— LUCILLE BALL

Stopping Negative Self-Talk

I don't know why, but I hear far more women than men using negative self-talk. So many women are quick to put themselves down. It's common, and it sucks. There's no good reason for it, and it needs to stop.

Well, one way to amp up your self-love is to *trash that trash talk*. Throw it away. Don't use it. From here on out, the rule is: Say NO to negative self-talk. What is negative self-talk? It's any self-talk that puts you down. It's language that doesn't make you sparkle or feel better. It's also any negativity you direct at other people, like judgments about them, or comments about things you don't like about them. It's all negative, and—here's the kicker—*it all impacts you.*

Do you think your life is crappy and wonder why? I'll tell you why... it's your negative self-talk that makes life ugly. It's always the reason. No matter what's going on around you, how you *respond* is what matters, and your self-talk determines how you respond.

If you want to have the best life, you must have the best self-talk. Because bad thoughts bring bad things, and disastrous thoughts bring disaster. It's like a law. When you think about crappy things, then that's your focus, and that's what your brain looks for, and that's what you'll find. In fact, that's all you'll see. So STOP it!

This starts with what you see in the mirror first thing! It starts with how you see yourself, how you see your face, how you see your style, how you see your body. Do you look at your naked body in the mirror and say, "I love you"? I'll bet most of the women reading this don't... I know I didn't used to.

This also means that you don't even joke about yourself. Don't joke and say, *"I'm such an idiot."* Don't joke and say, *"It's hard living in this body."* And for Christ's sake, don't joke and say, *"I'm fat."*

Don't do it. Just don't.

Because, trust me, your subconscious is listening. And it will do what you tell it. It makes your thoughts *real.* Your subconscious does not have a sense of humor. It doesn't understand jokes. It takes everything you say and think as a command, and then it tries to make it happen for you. So stop joking about your weight, or your "faults," or whatever else... because that's not how you love yourself. Find other ways to play and have fun.

I love a good sense of humor, but not at the expense of cracking unhealthy jokes about myself or others. What about self-deprecating humor? The definition of "deprecating" is *disapproval!* That's not what we're going for.

(Note: Self-deprecating humor can be nuanced, and there are cases where it comes from a position of high self-esteem, or is used well strategically. But when most people use it, they're chipping away at themselves little by little, and that's what we're talking about here, and putting an end to it.)

I know I might seem extreme, but I'll take an uplifting compliment about myself any day, over a negative joke I crack about myself or my abilities. When you're self-critical, there's no shimmer. And when you're not shimmering, you're not loving yourself enough, which means you're not radiating a positive vibe, and you're not manifesting your dream life.

- So let's turn down the negativity and turn up the positivity.
- Because we are *so worth it*.

Be Aware So You Can Care

To stop your negative self-talk, you must first become aware of it. And you do this by listening to yourself. Take a magnifying glass to your day, and pay attention to how you feel from one hour to the next, from one minute to the next. Seriously, do this: Set an *hourly* alarm during your waking hours to check in with your mind. When you pay attention to how you internally talk to yourself, you start to learn where to remove negative thoughts and inject more positive self-talk.

The fascinating thing is, most of us are much harsher on ourselves than we are to others. Even more fascinating, when we hear somebody we love speaking poorly about themselves, we jump to tell them *they're crazy*! Their words are poison in our ears! It's like swallowing glass! Imagine your son or daughter, or sister or brother, or mother or father, or best friend, saying terrible things about themselves. You'd intervene! You'd grab them by the shoulders and shake glittery sense into them, because you want to shake self-love into them. Well, guess what, my love? You need to do this for yourself!

Negative self-talk will do nothing to move you toward your dreams. It's harmful, and hurtful, and needs to be abolished 100% from your speech. You'll find that, as you start saying more loving things to yourself, you become more self-aware of all negative thinking. In no time, your new loving mindset will become your default, so keep showing up and doing your Lipstick Self-Talk. And any time negativity rears its monstrous head, just double down, and do your Lipstick Self-Talk even more.

Two Ways to STOP Negative Self-Talk

Method 1: Your Diamond Shovel

Why a shovel? Because, with this method, you're going to dig, dig, dig. The moment you catch yourself thinking or saying something negative about yourself, or your life, or your circumstances... you stop what you're doing. You grab your metaphorical diamond shovel, and you dig into the *why*.

Ask yourself: *Why do I feel this way?*

And then, whatever the answer is, dig deeper.

And why is that?

And you keep going. For each answer, you keep asking why, just like little kids do. *Why—Why—Why?*

You keep digging, asking yourself why. After a few times, you almost always find something you fear at the bottom of that hole. But here's the magic... once you get to the very bottom, that fear, that *why*... you realize it's not as devastating as you had thought. Sometimes, the thing you feared isn't actually scary at all.

For example, imagine a woman is at her job, and she wants to speak up about something, but she holds back and says nothing. She worries about what people would think. She's self-conscious. And so she keeps quiet. But fortunately, our heroine has been reading *Lipstick Self-Talk,* and she realizes that this is one of those moments, where she must get her diamond-plated shovel and dig.

She asks the first *why...* "*Why don't I speak up?*"

Her diamond shovel starts to sparkle as she realizes she doesn't speak up at work because she's afraid someone won't like her ideas. She's already identified a fear, but she keeps on digging. She asks... "*Why am I afraid of someone not liking my ideas?*" And she realizes she doesn't want people to think poorly of her. And the deeper she digs, the more brilliantly her diamond shovel sparkles.

"*Why am I afraid of people thinking poorly of me?*"

And she realizes that she's afraid she could lose her job. So again, she asks why. *Why am I afraid to lose my job?* And she realizes it's because she needs her job for money, and without money, she would be out on the street. *Diamond Shovel Sparkles!*

But then something amazing happens.

At this moment, she realizes that it's very unlikely that anything she would say might realistically lead to her getting fired. And if she did, she could always get another job. In fact, if push came to shove, she could always move in with her mom... there would be no sleeping on the street. Or she could bring in a roommate to help with money. She realizes there are a number of ways to handle that fear at the very bottom of the hole, and that it's never going to happen anyway.

So why is she afraid of speaking up?

In this light, she considers the upside. What if people like her suggestion? What if it leads to more respect? What if coming up with good ideas and being more assertive, over time, lead to more responsibilities? Or promotions?

So with her loving self-talk, she boosts her self-esteem, her confidence, and her self-love, and then she starts speaking up at work. She's empowered, and she can handle anything that happens. Her diamond shovel sparkles so bright, it's almost blinding. Its energy infuses her, empowers her, because as she has dug deep, she knows she has the answers within her. They were always there.

We are more often frightened than hurt; and we suffer more from imagination than from reality.

— SENECA

In the beginning of your self-love journey, you may find yourself using your diamond shovel a lot. It's the best way to dig deep into your soul to discover what drives your behaviors. *To find your compelling why.* But after a while, you find yourself using the diamond shovel less and less often. It's not that negative thoughts don't still pop up once in a while, but they're much less intrusive. And in these instances, you can tap into the next method: The Love Swap.

Method 2: The Love Swap

The brain can only think and feel one way at a time. You're not going to feel, say, love and fear at the same time. And you can use this incredible knowledge to your advantage. When you're experiencing a moment of negative self-talk, you want to interrupt that pattern *immediately*. I actually do this by clapping my hands, abruptly and loudly, two times. And it signals me to replace the negative words and thoughts with my positive words and thoughts. That's it.

In those moments when this felt hard to do, or it felt weird or strange, or it even made me question my sincerity about the positive words, I stuck with it anyway, and I replaced the words in my head with something like...

I am love, I am love, I am love...

OR

I am happy, I am happy, I am happy...

OR

I am safe, I am safe, I am safe...

OR

My life is wonderful, my life is wonderful, my life is wonderful...

I chose a simple line, and I repeated it over, and over, and over, sometime ten seconds, sometimes a minute or longer. And the craziest thing always happened! When I'm saying the positive self-talk, the negativity always gets snuffed out. *Poof.* It fades aways, and I immediately start to feel better.

The more you do it, the easier it gets. The first few times, it took a bit of effort. But the fifth time I did it, and the tenth, and the hundredth —well, I'm a pro now. I can shift my vibe on a dime, because I've trained my brain to do it. And you can, too.

Lipstick Self-Talk

I come from greatness. I attract greatness. I am greatness!

I trust my feelings. I trust my intuition.

I am healthy and sparkly.

I love my precious body.

I am a magnificent, radiant being.

Exercise

What is something you're afraid of? Write it down, and go through the Diamond Shovel exercise, asking "why?" multiple times to get at the root of the fear. Then, write down various reasons why the fear is overblown, incorrect, or not needed.

CHAPTER 6

FUN SELF-LOVE TIP: SHOE LOVE NOTES

Self-care is giving the world the best you instead of what's left of you.

— Katie Reed

Here's a delightful little self-love activity that's perfect for women because a lot of women have a lot of shoes, right? But even if you don't, like me, this self-love tip is phenomenal, and it works no matter how many pairs of shoes you have.

1. Get out a pad of sticky notes.
2. Write a little love note or affirmation to yourself on one sticky note for each pair of shoes in your closet.
3. Fold your sticky notes and stick one of them into one of the shoes for each pair.
4. How fun… someday in the future—days, weeks, months, or years from now—to pick up a pair of shoes and see that you left yourself a little love note.

Love notes like…

I am worthy.

I am power.

I am strong.

I am flexible.

I am sexy.

Amazing woman, that's me!

I am love.

I am wonderful.

I love me.

I love my life.

I am generous.

I am kind.

Watch me go!

CHAPTER 7

THIS IS YOUR BRAIN ON
LIPSTICK SELF-TALK

*Whatever we plant in our subconscious mind, and nourish with repetition
and emotion, will one day come to reality.*

— EARL NIGHTINGALE

Self-talk has been used in cognitive therapy for decades, with a
proven track record for helping with depression, anxiety, PTSD,
eating disorders, and more, as well as goal achievement and high
performance by people like professional athletes, pilots, and business
executives. What's so exciting is the cool stuff going on under the
hood (inside your skull), when you first utter the positive words... the
"proof" of how this magicky-feeling stuff works.

I described earlier how we have thoughts and behaviors based on
past programming and wiring in our brain. It got that way from years
of repetition, amplified by the level of emotional intensity at the time.
That same idea, combining repetition and emotional intensity, is how
you'll change your brain and life going forward. It's called "neuro-
plasticity," which means that your brain can change (even if it feels

impossible), rewiring itself, and changing how you think. In other words, changing *you*. You'll use Lipstick Self-Talk to do this.

Let's geek out on this for a minute. Do remember those ads back in the day designed to scare you away from drugs? *"This is your brain. This is your brain on drugs"*? Well, I like to talk about the brain in a positive way, regarding positive self-talk, with the same idea. I say, *"This is your brain. And this is your brain on positive self-talk."*

Your brain on Lipstick Self-Talk is full of glittery, rich, saucy, awesomeness. Why? Because positive self-talk literally, truly, feels good when you do it. Because, when you utter the words, your brain swims in feel-good chemicals. When you use your positive self-talk, it creates an uplifted emotional state. It creates a sense of accomplishment. And this feels good. It feels exciting.

When you use your self-talk to control your mind, your aim is to accomplish two things:

1. The self-talk contains affirmations about you and the person you want to become. For this book, that's a self-loving, high self-esteem, confident person.
2. The other aim of self-talk is to manifest your goals and dreams.

If you look at these two, you'll notice they're actually both a form of goal. Whether it's a goal to have more self-love in your life, or a goal to manifest something in your life, such as physical health or prosperity. **These are goals.** And our brains are designed to reward us with good feelings when we set goals. So, the minute you start your self-talk, you're automatically stating goals, intentions, and desires. And our brains reward us for doing this with feel-good brain chemicals like dopamine and serotonin.

But then, something else happens! Your self-talk not only builds a foundation of self-worth with these beautiful intentions, but there's also a part of your brain called the *reticular activating system* that takes action *on your behalf.* It basically sits there, waiting and listening for direction from you. It pays attention to your words, because your words direct your focus. I think of the reticular activating system like having a little wizard behind a little curtain in my brain. The wizard sits there with a clipboard and a fancy, pink fountain pen waiting for my direction. And when I give it the direction, which is my self-talk, the wizard jots down notes so it can help make whatever I've said come true.

- If my focus is good, the wizard helps me see more good. In myself, my life, and the world around me.
- If my focus is trash, the wizard helps me see more trash!

The wizard (my reticular activating system) doesn't care what my focus is, it just takes the order and helps me make that focus become more prominent in my life. If your thoughts are good thoughts, your brain focuses on good things. It makes things catch your attention that match your "good" focus. Not just on rainbows and puppies, but on alternatives and practical solutions to your problems—the things that will make real differences in your life.

Let me give you an example...

- Imagine you want a beautiful, romantic, ride-off-into-the-sunset love. This is more likely to happen with someone who shares your values, right? And so you think about this love that you want, and you come up with details about this person that would make a good fit for you: a sense of humor, a supportive person, a person who loves nature, good with kids, etc. And they're good details, loving details, because it's how you think about your own life.
- And then you go about your day. Perhaps the world has twenty potential partners on the immediate horizon, but the ones that shimmer and catch your eye *are the ones that match your focus.* Your reticular activating system (your little wizard)

can actually make you see things, or you hear coffee shop conversations that you would have otherwise filtered out! Let's say one of these potential partners loves camping and comedies and is looking for a loving, supportive person, like you. You see and hear details you might have otherwise missed... you tune into the person's *vibe*. This person shimmered and caught your attention because you had a defined focus, and it was fueled with self-love. (Even if you're not seeking romance, just go with me here... the same idea applies to anything you seek in life.)

- Now imagine another person who wants a romantic, cinematic love, but she doesn't love herself very much, and she doesn't even know what she likes in life. Heck, she barely knows herself. And so she thinks poorly about herself, frequently criticizes and downplays her passions and achievements. She thinks she'll never find this wonderful, romantic love, because she wonders, who would ever love her? Well, with *this* focus and self-talk, the brain still goes to work and makes certain partners shimmer on the horizon. It does her bidding. But what's "shimmering" here are bad matches, not likely to succeed. They fit her negative attitudes, but that's not who she really is, because deep down, she wants to love herself. We all do.

So, the question is... are your thoughts setting you up for magical living? Are you directing your brain's little wizard to help you see the things that will help you live your most loving life? Or not? When you're scared or feeling unworthy, you attract the wrong people and wrong experiences. The wrong results. But with the *right stuff*... well, that's rainbow living. That's true power.

Our brains are right there, waiting for us to use them to the fullest benefit. And when we focus our self-talk on positive things, our brains help us make it happen.

This *Feeeeels* Really Great

Back to those incredible, feel-good brain chemicals I mentioned...

- Your brain secretes different feel-good chemicals for different things. When you set a goal or intention, which is exactly what your Lipstick Self-Talk is (self-love goals and intentions), dopamine is secreted because you have set a goal. This neurochemical gives you feelings of pleasure, desire, and motivation. It's pure awesome.

But wait, there's more!

- Then, every step you take toward that goal, such as doing your *daily* Lipstick Self-Talk, or doing loving things for yourself throughout the day, or taking steps toward any goal you set, your brain knows this. And your brain rewards you with more dopamine every time you take a step. *That means more good feelings.*

But wait there's even more! :)

- Serotonin, another feel-good chemical, gets secreted when you feel good about doing something, like when you feel pride. It's a beautiful, calm feeling that *you're strong enough* to meet your needs and desires, despite any conditions in your life or the world.

That's why this whole ritual feels so great. *It's all about the feeeeels!* It's what keeps us coming back to our positive self-talk every day. It's about reveling in those luminous, feel-good neurochemicals and attracting the things that match our energy. Between the feel-good chemicals and the reticular activating system (your awesome little brain wizard), you can use positive self-talk to feel amazing *and* make your dreams come true. You will live your most beautiful life.

A Big BUT

There's a trick to this process, however. And that's the "big but." This all works like a finely tuned machine ... BUT only if you do it every day! You have to make your positive self-talk *the* priority. Think of it like a muscle... the more you exercise that muscle, the stronger it gets. When you do it every day, all of that devotion adds up. Continually building you, adding layers to your self-love foundation.

If you have the ability to love, love yourself first.

— CHARLES BUKOWSKI

Lipstick Self-Talk

My brain helps me love myself more every day.

I focus on what makes me shine like the sun.

My mind is my superpower.

My love is like wildfire inside of me.

I love myself, just as I am.

Exercise

Write down three actions of self-love you will take this week. Now get your calendar and add them there, too. For extra magic, send me a message on Instagram (CoffeeSelfTalk) or post in our amazing Facebook group about what you're doing for your self-love this week.

CHAPTER 8

THE OXYGEN MASK

If you aren't good at loving yourself, you will have a difficult time loving anyone, since you'll resent the time and energy you give another person that you aren't even giving to yourself.

— BARBARA DE ANGELIS

This is one of the most important chapters in the book. I saved it until now so you didn't freak out.

Buckle up.

We're diving deep and doing what we should've been doing all our life—but never had the courage to do it: We're officially *putting ourselves first.*

Let me ask you...

- Do you tie your self-worth to the happiness or well-being of others?
- Do you find your self-worth tied to doing well at work?
- Do you place productivity before your happiness?

- Do you feel guilty when you do things for yourself or when you take a break and kick up your feet?
- Do you do things for others even when you feel like saying no?

Or let's be even more honest...

- Do you put others first because it makes you feel important to do so?
- Do you find your worth from helping others instead of helping yourself?

Time. To. Stop.

It's time to put on your own oxygen mask first.

Why This Is *Mission Self-Love* Critical

When I decided to write a book about self-love, the metaphor of the oxygen mask leaped front and center in my mind. As I mentioned earlier, too many women were writing to me saying they wanted to do Coffee Self-Talk, but they had a two-year-old, or other obligations, and they didn't have the five minutes to do it. Do you know what this is? It's the woman putting on her child's oxygen mask first.

But. There is a vital reason why the airlines tell you to put on your own mask first.

You cannot help others if you are incapacitated.

You cannot help others if you are sick.

You cannot help others if you are weak.

You cannot help others if you are run down.

You cannot help others if you are dead!

The Answer: You must love yourself—*first*—before you can properly love someone else, whether it's your partner, a child, an elderly parent, your business, or a friend.

But, Kristen, isn't it selfish to love ourselves first?

Here's the counterintuitive truth. Loving yourself is not selfish. In fact, it's the opposite. If you don't love yourself, you can't fully be there for others, including your children! I admit, that's hard to swallow at first. We want our offspring to survive, and that makes us inclined to put them first.

But that's the kicker... if you're unconscious (or exhausted, or sick, or whacked out by stress), it's harder to help them. You can't help others unless you've helped yourself. And when you take care of yourself first, you both survive. In fact, you both thrive.

I love this quote from Maya Angelou:

> *I don't trust people who don't love themselves and tell me*
> *'I love you.'... There is an African saying:*
> *"Be careful when a naked person offers you a shirt."*

It Comes Down to This

If you don't love yourself, you come to life half-assed. You're tired, weak, and frazzled, so you can't be there for your kids, spouse, and others. the way they deserve. If you're in a romantic relationship, you can't connect with your mate when you're headachy, stressed out, or a zombie running on an empty tank. And you can't do a good job at work if you can't show up with energy and focus.

If you don't love yourself, you won't properly care for yourself. This makes you more likely to get sick. Lose energy. And feel poopy-blah. You just can't be an awesome parent or spouse like this.

Before I started my epic love affair with ME, I showed up each day less patient and short-tempered. I complained more. I whined more. I was annoyed by minor things. This presented a bad example for my daughter, and when she asked for help, I was distracted and didn't shower her with the attention she deserved. Ugh... the times I snapped at her like an angry, over-worked alligator... But not anymore!

This Ain't Your Average Self-Love

To truly love yourself, and be a pro at it, self-love can't just be a tiny part of the day when you focus on yourself. *It's a lifestyle.* You must value yourself *and everything you do.*

And by living this way, you change the lives of everybody around you. That's the crazy thing about this... most people (especially women) live it ass-backwards. **When you put other people first, nobody wins.** But if put your own self-love first, then you come to the table of life—to your day, to your family, to the world—better able to help and do an amazing job.

- If you want to change your family, work on yourself.
- If you want to change the world, work on yourself.

We must first succeed alone that we may enjoy our success together.

— Henry David Thoreau

Now You Know

Thoreau also wrote that, "once a person willfully makes a choice to act in one way, or refrain from doing something else, that decision puts everyone else in a position to now make that decision for themselves, too." This idea blew my mind. What you don't know, you don't know. But when you do know better, you do better, and so do those around you.

When I *chose to be happy* **during the COVID-19 pandemic** (yes, you read that right—I chose to have a *good time* in lockdown), it was not an act of self-delusion, it was an act of self-love. And this spilled over to others in my life. It showed everybody else I came into contact with that they, too, had a choice: They could choose to be happy, or unhappy. Perhaps they didn't know there was a choice, but once they saw me living a certain way, they knew they had a choice. I'm not dismissing the suffering that many people endured. But my family and I all got sick, and I still chose self-love and positive self-talk to keep my happiness as my focus.

I was staking a claim to another way to live, and I was not letting the conditions of the world steal my joy. I was wild and willful when I was happy during the pandemic. How did I do it? It was very easy. I simply decided my happiness did not depend on there being no pandemic. It was a choice. A choice to be happy.

Further...

- My happiness does not depend on the success of my work.
- My happiness does not depend on my spouse's attitude.
- My happiness does not depend on whether or not my parents get along.
- My happiness does not depend on whether my child does well in school. Or dare I say, my happiness does not even depend on my child's complete happiness.

It's a tough pill to swallow, but fascinating, right?

This doesn't mean that you don't strive like hell to help others find their happy, or that your heartstrings never get tugged on when someone in your life is sad or upset. It just means I know I'll be able to help someone *more* if I'm coming from a positive place. I also know we're all responsible for our own happiness, and we cannot make it dependent on other people, even our children. It's not fair to ourselves, and frankly, it's not fair to our children.

In fact, we wouldn't want their happiness dependent on us! So why, oh why, do we think it's okay for our happiness to be dependent on them when we'd admonish someone for making their happiness dependent on us?

Think about that.

I know. I know. This isn't an easy adjustment for everyone to make, at least, not without chewing on it first. And perhaps the bigger problem is that a lot of people don't put their desires or happiness *even on the same level as their kids'*. Moms especially. But having this new mindset changed the way I navigated my life as a mom.

There's no rule written anywhere that says having a family means putting your happiness on hold for 18 years!

I like what Pamela Druckerman writes in her book, *Bringing Up Bébé*, regarding something as simple as bedtime for kids: "French parents are strict about enforcing bedtime. They treat adult time not as an occasional, hard-won privilege, but as a basic human need."

I wish I had read that when my daughter was a baby. *Adult time is a basic human need.* Let that sink in.

Teaching Others to Fish

How will our children even learn what self-love is if we don't show them? Imagine this... imagine teaching your children to love themselves, and imagine how that would influence the way they grow up. Imagine the expansive life they can have when they're confident, happy, and whole. Able to stand on their own. You might think your children love themselves, but they probably aren't loving themselves as much as you think, *if you're not loving yourself.*

My daughter started loving herself more when I started loving myself more. I had always expected her to love herself, and I assumed she did, because of course she's worthy! She's a child! But how can she understand what it's like to love herself if I'm not setting an example? *I need to be the role model.* Otherwise, my child would grow up like the former me. Did I want that? Did I want my daughter to grow up sacrificing her own happiness for her partner, or her boss, or friends? Do I want my daughter to grow up thinking it's normal and okay to be tired and rundown? A doormat? No effin' way!

What Does This Mean?

It means you take the time to love yourself like you really mean it. Maybe it's ten minutes, or twenty minutes, or an hour *every day*, and you do things that recharge your batteries. You prioritize your self-care and happiness.

For me, that's...

- My self-talk rituals, because those rituals help me live my most magical life.
- I tell myself I love myself multiple times a day.
- I exercise five days a week. Moving my body keeps me energized, and it's good for my brain, and heart, and lungs, and muscles, and bones.
- I buy myself little luxuries.
- I watch a fun TV show when I'm tired and I want to relax.
- I'm self-aware enough to know right away when *I need more of me* in my life. And I act on it.
- I go to bed early.
- I often say "no" to others and "yes" to me.

But it's not always black and white. It's not always *me-me-me* and no one else... but my self-loving lifestyle has become a general guideline for me. I now make family decisions on a case-by-case basis, realizing I no longer keep myself second, or last, all the time. I did that for years, and it nearly destroyed me as I tried to be the perfect mom.

The Hard Truth

If you always put your children's needs first, the reality smacks them hard when they get into the real world and see that not everybody treats them this way.

You support others, sure. You love, and help, and guide, of course. But not at the expense of you all the time. Not at the expense of you never finding even five minutes for your own soul, your own growth. Because that which doesn't grow, dies. Yes, a part of you will die. And when the time comes that the kids leave the nest, you might not even know who you are anymore.

But...

When you soar in self-love, you become a better mom, a better wife, a better teacher, a better friend, a better neighbor, and a better lover.

And this teaches everyone around you how to do the same.

The Room Divider

Ernest Hemingway would spend hours writing in an uninterrupted setting, and what a blessing that was for him. He'd write in a quaint café in Paris, at a little table, and he'd have his wine there. Sipping it. Writing with his pen and paper. And he was not interrupted... because his wife was home with the baby. He had freedom to do his clearest, best thinking.

Any artist will tell you that interruption disrupts your flow. It can kill creativity. I know I can't write if I'm constantly interrupted, because my flow gets jarred out of whack. So here's another instance when I had to take control and put myself and my art first, and it was an act of self-love for me to do it. I had to let my family know I'm not the only one who answers questions. I had to tell my daughter, "You don't always have to come to me. You can ask your dad questions. You can

Google questions. You can text message your nana if you have questions."

So, when I set out to make sure I had time by myself, I used a room divider. Literally. And when I was working or creating or writing, there was a rule: I was not to be interrupted. Unless "your hair is on fire." You get my drift, emergencies were obvious exceptions.

I took action to protect my writing time. My "me" time. And do you know what? The world went on. My daughter survived. My husband jumped in to help, in fact, teaching my daughter to do things for herself that I used to do for her, like making grilled cheese sandwiches. I had to make a change because I had fallen for the idea that it's the woman who should be available to help others at all times. I lived that way for years, and I finally said, *enough is enough*. I put up the room divider, and it worked.

So what is it that you can do? Here are some suggestions.

- **Outsourcing is a beautiful thing.** If you have a two-year-old at home, and you want five or ten minutes to do your self-talk or nurture yourself, then get a special toy that they only have access to during this five or ten minutes. Call it the *Mommy Time Toy*, and just wait and see how much your little one will look forward to you taking Mommy Time!
- **Consider letting your child play on a tablet** for five or ten minutes while you take special time for yourself and for your self-love. I used to be one of those moms who freaked out and wouldn't let my daughter use an iPad if she was too young. But, oh my god, when I finally allowed it, it was like the clouds parted and relaxation rained down. And you can bet that I didn't let guilt kill the buzz. Technology is a wonderful babysitter, and I was happy to use it smartly to give me time to become a better mom. Naturally, be mindful about setting limits here. (Tip: Setting a timer helps with enforcing screen time limits.)

- **Outsource other things like laundry or cooking** once in a while. And do your self-love then.
- **Look at your schedule,** and find pockets of time where you might have been wasting it and could've been using it to your advantage.
- **Enlist the help of others.** Goodness, I remember the times when I didn't ask my husband for help because I saw it as a failure on my part, or I felt like he was too busy making money, and I wasn't working as much, so I shouldn't bother him. Now I don't hesitate to manage the household like a badass CEO, which means delegating tasks.
- **Get a room divider or a "Do Not Disturb" sign for the door.**

I'll be honest, I didn't just do it overnight. I started small. I had to ease my way into it because I wasn't used to this new way of thinking. Things like asking my husband, *"Can you please put away the dishes?* He was happy to help. In fact, what I learned is people like to help! But they can't help if you don't ask. And so we must realize it's good to ask for help, and it's good to take time for self-love, because we make the world a better place when we do.

Lipstick Self-Talk

I'm taking care of myself, from morning to night.

Everything is going so very right.

Loving myself is freedom.

I deserve to glitter, sparkle, and shine.

I matter. 'Nuff said.

Exercise

It's time to put these ideas into action and put on your own oxygen mask first. What are some ways you can start living your self-love life-style? Write them down here.

CHAPTER 9

FUN SELF-LOVE TIP: FINE CHINA & NIGHTIES

Be yourself, because an original is worth more than a copy.

— Suzy Kassem

Sometimes the smallest things can have a big impact. And my self-love tip here is:

Use your fancy dishes.

(Or buy yourself a nightgown. More on this in a minute.) When I was young, my mom taught me there was no reason to "save" the special dishes for special occasions. Why? Because every day is a special occasion. She believed that presentation of food was always an opportunity to enjoy life. In fact, it's a small act of self-love.

Back when I was a competitive bodybuilder in college (more on that in a later chapter), she used to make my food for me, which was *a lot* of boring chicken breasts. But Mom would make it more enticing, because she'd use our best dishes to serve my plain, rubbery chicken.

She'd sprinkle green herbs on the plate to decorate it. She'd even serve my chocolate protein shake in a wine glass!

And you know what? It tasted better. *And I felt special.*

This taught me the importance of presentation when it comes to food, and she said we were worth using the good stuff on a regular basis. And with that... I recommend the same for you. Take out your nice wine glass or goblet, your lovely, fine bone china plates, and eat on them for no other reason than "you're worth it."

If you don't have any particularly nice china, then get online and buy yourself a silky-soft nightgown. I found a great one on Amazon.com for about twenty bucks, and every time I slip it over my shoulders, I feel a little wave of happiness pass through me, and I think about the act of self-love I'm doing by treating myself to a little something special.

CHAPTER 10

PERMISSION TO BE YOU

Today you are you! That is truer than true!

There is no one alive who is you-er than you!

Shout loud, 'I am lucky to be what I am!'

— DR. SEUSS

Today is about embracing you. All of you. There is no more hiding. And no more apologies. It's time to love you. Love your quirks and the weird little habits that make you smile. If something lights you up for good reason, then have fun. If you want to believe in fairies and unicorns and magic, then do it! I personally let myself get jazzed about things like that, fantastical ideas that expand my imagination. I love coming up with brazen, silly ideas for inventions, no shyness or blushing. I love what Anita Moorjani says, *"The last time someone said I was delusional, I almost fell off my unicorn."*

I give myself permission to do, and feel, and think any way I want. I believe in magic, and energy, and awe, and I stuff my days full of, *"Holy Shit! That's extraordinary! Look what just happened?"* Even if it's merely having the perfect parking spot open just as I'm pulling into a packed parking lot.

No Apologies

Make no apologies for being who you are, or for loving yourself and choosing yourself first. There's no need to wince if your desk or home isn't super tidy and organized, at least, not if you like it that way. Don't apologize for the amount of space you use, no matter your size. You are you, and you are worthy of love.

Authenticity is the name of the game, and when you're true to yourself, every bone and cell in your body will glow with delight.

You are to be you.

To do you.

And be the best you that you can be...

... otherwise, the world will have one less shining light.

And I want your light shining. We all do.

Whatever comes up in life, you'll feel your way through it with love. Whatever needs to be said, you can say it. Permission to be you. Permission for all of us to shine and be who we are destined to be. If someone else doesn't understand, that's fine, they don't have to. We just keep on shining.

If you want French fries on your pizza, then pile them on. Shaved parmesan, on top of whipped cream, on top of chocolate chip ice cream?

Go for it.

You do you.

I'll love you for it, for expanding my mind with your ideas.

You'll love yourself for it, too. You'll feel like dancing, so happy to be free.

We have infinite options in our life's path. Life is one humongous, tantalizing buffet. Take a taste, anytime, on anything, and explore. Do you like it? Great, keep going. Do you not like that taste? No problem, skip it, trash it, or pivot, and try something new. Permission to be you.

My mother told me to be a lady. And for her, that meant be your own person, be independent.

— RUTH BADER GINSBURG

From Playing It Scared... To Badass Boldness

I used to play it safe, years ago when I was blogging full time. I was careful about what I said, rarely revealing any strong opinions. I didn't want to deal with conflict. I had passions I believed in, but I lacked confidence. I didn't feel worthy enough to share my thoughts because I didn't have a PhD in the subject. I was afraid that, if I stated an opinion I hadn't thoroughly researched, people would attack me.

It was a small way to live.

It turns out, when I limited what I shared, I limited my life experience. I didn't consider that nobody knows everything. I could have put my thoughts out into the world, with confidence, despite not having all the answers—and even stating this disclaimer as my battle cry. There's nothing wrong with not knowing it all. In fact, what better way to learn than to sprinkle your thoughts like wildflower seeds and start a discussion? Who knows what beauties might take root and blossom?

All that changed. Now that I've built my foundation of self-love, bold confidence is my new norm. It was the natural reward of my newfound worthiness. No more limited, small living. It was time to get loud, bold, and playful. Now I throw my hands up and laugh when I don't have an answer. I screw my eyeballs together when dancing with the unknown.

When you love yourself, it becomes easier to be your *true* self. And it feels pretty badass.

Finding Your Own Frequency

Take a moment and find your own frequency—your *vibe*—through the stillness. It's there, I promise. (It's always there.) How do you feel when you close your eyes and feel your heart? Do you feel loud and pizzazzy? Do you feel soft and squishy? Do you feel glittery and sexy? When you are your authentic self, you'll attract the right people to you, creating the most magical expansion in your life.

You are life. You are energy. You are a force. We are literally made of stardust, so *shine, baby, shine.*

You are you. I am not you. You are not me. We don't want to all be the same. How boring that would be, right? There'd be less innovation, less art, less of everything exciting. So, let's make a deal. I'll do me, because only I can do me. You do you, because only you can do you. And when I shine, you shine! And when you shine, I shine!

Permission to Evolve

And guess what? We all change. We evolve. You're under no obligation to be the same person you were last year. Or a month ago, or even twenty minutes ago. You have the right to grow. You have the right to change your mind. You have the right to evolve. You have the right to be a certain way today, and tomorrow, and something different next week.

You have permission to create a new you, brilliant and sparkling, every moment of the day.

I'll leave you with this gem from comedian Whitney Cummings:

People-pleasing is a form of assholery... because you're not pleasing anybody—you're just making them resentful because you're being disingenuous, and you're also not giving them the dignity of their own experience [by assuming] they can't handle the truth.

Lipstick Self-Talk

I am authentically me, and I love me.

I focus on what lights me up.

I am meant to have big fun!

I embrace my space. I'm bold. I'm brave.

I have permission to be me.

Exercise

What expands your energy? What things make you feel larger than life, excited, and in awe? Why do these things do that for you? And how can you have more of those things in your life?

_____

_____

_____

_____

_____

_____

CHAPTER 11

RESPECT YOUR CHOICES

All good things are wild and free.

— Henry David Thoreau

In Chapter 3, I talked about self-respect. We're going to expand upon that theme here, specifically, respecting your *choices*.

Have you ever felt pressured to do something? Perhaps it's a pushy salesperson, or well-intentioned advice from a friend. If you don't want to do the thing they're recommending, but you want to soften your rejection, you can always just say:

Thank you for the information. I'll think about it.

No one can blame you for taking the time to think something over. It's a sign of prudence and maturity.

That's one of the best bits of advice I can give whenever you feel lost or confused or pressured. Simply say: *Thank you, I appreciate your input. I'll think about it and get back to you.*

Buy yourself time. Because, when you feel pressured to do something, and you go ahead and do it, your self-love takes a hit. Because you feel like you didn't stand up for yourself, or you didn't take the time to process something that required thought.

You have the right to think about things. You have permission to ponder, so you can make the best possible decisions. And really, if you feel pressured, there's a good chance it wasn't meant to be anyway.

Decision-Making Tip

One day, when I was deciding on whether or not to attend a seminar, a sassy girlfriend of mine advised, "If it's not a *f*ck yeah*, then it's a *no*." I chuckled at her language, but immediately after, I was like, *You're right!* That's a great way to make decisions.

Or, at least, make this your first filter, with an option to think on it and change your mind if it makes sense. So, if it's not a *f*ck yeah*, then it's either a no, or it's a *need to think about it*. It's okay to think about things, no matter what it is... buying that pair of shoes, going on that date, adopting that kitten. (On second thought, just adopt the kitten. No pressure.) 😊

Always Apologizing?

And what's with always feeling like we need to apologize for saying "no" to something? I'm thinking about mostly women here, because so often, women feel the need to apologize for things. Where does that come from? It's time for it to stop. Why can't we just say, *"Yeah, um, no thanks."* I think men are pretty good at just saying no to things. I take inspiration from Phoebe on the TV show, *Friends*. When asked if she wanted to do something, she said sweetly, "Oh thanks, I would, except I don't want to." *You go, Phoebe!*

I know, I know... we want to be polite.

We don't want to come off as rude.

I get it.

But it bears asking the question: Do *you* apologize a lot? Do you have an energy that's fearful, or scared, or do you feel like you should apologize because your "no thanks" isn't enough? It's time to examine all these apologies. And let's be clear, I'm not saying you don't apologize if you've made a mistake. Apologies are great in that instance. I'm talking about the knee-jerk reaction to always apologize just because you say "no" to something.

If your heart is really against doing something, or you really just don't want to do something because it doesn't feel right, or it doesn't bring you joy, or because you'd rather watch paint dry, then why are you apologizing? Are you not feeling strong and certain? Or are you just truly super-polite? I mean, you can still say no sweetly... but you don't always have to say you're sorry when you do it.

The Big Picture

Some situations are unique. And sure, there will be times you feel good offering an apology when you turn something down. I'm not saying never do it. I'm merely suggesting that you start to take stock of how often you apologize. Because, frankly, when I apologize just to be polite, for something that I'm saying no to, I immediately feel like I've not been as assertive as I should. And that chips away a little bit of my self-respect. When you value yourself, you respect your decisions, and you don't need to apologize for making decisions that other people might not like.

Instead, I like to say something pleasant like, "No thank you, but thank you for the opportunity." It's just as pleasant, but I didn't have to apologize when there's nothing to apologize for, and my self-esteem walks a little bit taller as a result.

Lipstick Self-Talk

I respect my ideas and my choices.

I can change my mind at any time.

I am my own truth.

I listen to my intuition. It speaks to me.

I take my time whenever I need.

Exercise

What are three ways you're going to find 10-minute pockets for self-love in your week?

....

....

....

CHAPTER 12

A SELF-LOVE AFFAIR TO REMEMBER

To love yourself right now, just as you are, is to give yourself heaven. Don't wait until you die. If you wait, you die now. If you love, you live now.

— ALAN COHEN

Self-love enhances the senses, illuminates the eyes, sharpens the hearing, brightens tastes. It quickens your steps, making them lighter, making you feel brighter. It relaxes the space between your brows, it steadies your hands... it protects your soul. It keeps your spirit young. Self-love makes you curious. It leans into exploration. It makes you see things, people, and places differently.

Many people might think of these things about a love affair with a romantic partner, but no, I'm talking about having this kind of love with *yourself*. Your self-love is the most magnificent love affair in the universe. You take it with you wherever you go.

The depth of your self-love determines the depth of your life experience.

If you don't have self-love, you go through life with a tank half-full, living half-alive. But with self-love, you're never confused, and your choices are clear. Your powers of intuition brim with sparkle, and it's so easy to access. It's like being on a permanent honeymoon, with you.

Self-love is the measure of your life, of your joy.

To be in love with your own heart, and your own mind, is the most beautiful experience. Self-love can be like a best friend and a lover. Like in a whirlwind romance, where your partner looks at you across a candlelit table and says, *"I love you so much."* Well... *that's* what I am to myself.

When I started on my self-love journey, I wanted to look in the mirror and feel that same level of rich intimacy *with myself*. **A real love affair.** And I wanted to be my own best friend. My *Bestie*. The one who high-fives herself, pumps herself up, and has her own back. It doesn't matter what happens in my day, or if I wake up feeling "off." I can look at myself in the mirror and say, *I love you*, and my breathing becomes calm and collected.

That's what I'm talking about when I say "self-love."

That's because love is the foundation of the magical mind you're cultivating. The relationship we have with our own selves is what everything else in our life is built upon. Do you see what I mean? It allows everything else to get built strongly *and stay strong*... from your relationships, to your health, to your career, to your life experiences.

Just like the foundation of a real house. Would you knowingly buy a house with a foundation that's crumbling or made from inferior materials? Of course not. You know that anything you build on a weak foundation will collapse. If not immediately, then eventually. Cracks will appear first, then they get bigger, until eventually other parts of the house come down in a crash.

The life you want can only be shimmer-shiny gold with a fabulous, rock-solid foundation. Do you want a life filled with success, magic, smiling, strength, love, and resilience? It first requires loving yourself as the core.

Start Loving Yourself All Day

We get busy with life, and we start doing things. Sometimes, we start out strong in the morning, and we're full of love for ourselves. Then, sometimes, something happens that pinches you with anxiety, or frustration, or self-doubt. During such times, the goal is to keep the *I love myself* love affair running all day long.

With practice and repetition, this experience becomes your default. But you have to do the work—the repetition. Make it a priority. With enough practice, I programmed my mind such that, whenever my mood started to dip, I simply said, "I love me." Short and sweet, under my breath, and I felt better. It became reflexive and effortless.

Every time I go to the bathroom, I look in the mirror, and another opportunity presents itself to maintain my self-love vibe. I look at myself in the mirror and say, *"Hi there, I'm having a great day."* I even wink at myself or blow a kiss. Sometimes I even give myself a fist bump in the mirror!

Yep, it feels super corny at first, but only the first few times. Then, you start to feel excitement about loving yourself, and then it's just flat-out *the new you.* The more you repeat your loving words for yourself, the faster you'll reprogram your subconscious mind.

I didn't fall in love with myself in one day. It wasn't love at first sight, though I wish it had been. It took repeated meetings in the bathroom, in the mirror. Just staring at myself, curious as to why I didn't see what others claimed to see, wondering if I could actually love myself the way I dreamed. I kept up my self-talk. I kept showing up, day after day. I was persistent. *Tenacious* was my middle name. I chose to honor myself, and you should too. I chose to not be frozen by the past, and so will you.

A Bedtime Love Story

At night, when you're in the bathroom getting ready for bed, tell yourself a little loving bedtime story. If your day wasn't everything you wanted, say *"It's okay, no worries, I love myself, and tomorrow is a new day."* Or, if your day was awesome, say, *"Yay! I had a great day. I love me, and there's more of that coming tomorrow. I'm so excited!"*

Then... when you're lying in bed, it's the perfect time to continue programming your subconscious. As you fall asleep, repeat over and over, *I love myself. I love my life.* A little mantra, a little prayer, a beautiful little self-love affair to remember. Just for you.

Lipstick Self-Talk

Dear Me, I love you. Love, Me.

I am destined for magnificence. I am a master manifester.

I trust the magic of my self-love.

I was born worthy. We all were.

I have fun being me, because life is a party.

Exercise

Take some time to get to know yourself better. Answer the following questions:

What are your favorite books and why?

....

....

....

If you could travel anywhere for one month, where would you go and why?

....

....

....

What are five things that instantly make you smile?

....

....

....

What really *matters* to you in life?

....

....

....

CHAPTER 13

CRAZY BODY IMAGE & BEAUTY

The words you speak become the house you live in.

— HAFIZ

I was in my early 20s, in a bodybuilding contest. I was on stage, holding my pose, looking into the blinding lights. My body fat was under 10%, and I was on display for the audience and judges in my super tiny, royal blue, sequined "posing" bikini-style suit. It was my fourth competition of the year, which meant I'd spent many, many months with my clothes fitting me perfectly as I trained and dieted from competition to competition.

But on stage, under the glare of the lights, what was I dreaming about? The two slabs of ribs and half dozen donuts I'd polish off after the competition. Yes, I really would eat six donuts. Sometimes more. Bingeing was common after competitions. It was even encouraged because it meant we'd put on some weight for a few days, boost our spirits (from temporarily not depriving ourselves), and then we'd start the cycle of losing the water and fat all over again, another 16 weeks of dieting and pumping iron for the next show.

This was pretty easy for me, though. I grew up in a household that was no stranger to dieting. Dexatrim was a common item in Mom's grocery cart. Her husband at the time used to give her a disapproving look if she reached for a second piece of crusty Italian bread.

All of this—diets, competition, perfect waistlines—eventually took its toll on my psyche, and so it's no surprise that I suffered from eating disorders. (But hey, it wasn't *all* the time, just occasional starving and bingeing and vomiting... no problem, right? Wrong. Rationalizing is dangerous. It was a very big problem.)

Well, those intermittent eating disorders eventually morphed into what's called "orthorexia," an unhealthy obsession with healthy eating. I denied that it was a problem for a decade, even to the point of convincing myself that orthorexia was a good thing, a badge of honor. A bogus, made-up label that unhealthy people invented because they couldn't manage to be as disciplined as diehards like me. But boy, was I ever wrong. It took years for me to realize that my "healthy" habits were taking a serious toll on my health because of all the stress that came along with it.

What Does All This Mean?

Earlier in the book, I talked about the wiring our brains receive from childhood. Between the obsession for staying in shape at all costs as a teen, to entering a sport that required an extreme devotion to bodily perfection, I had a lot of self-image problems. Anything less than perfect caused me to harshly criticize myself, and I got so accustomed to having my clothes fit a certain way that I became uncomfortable in my own skin. I couldn't love my body unless it was perfect, and I constantly, constantly judged myself. This was my messed-up value system. Which, unfortunately, led to judging others...

Judging Others

Excessive judging of others is a sign of a fragile ego and a lack of self-love. When we do it, we're implicitly comparing them to ourselves, propping up our own self-image at the other person's expense. (I say "excessively" because some judging is necessary. Such as when deciding whether to trust somebody, or when hiring someone, or deciding if we want a person in our lives, etc.)

I confess. I used to judge people. I'm not talking harsh, finger-pointing judgments because of people's socioeconomic status, politics, etc.—but I'd make petty little micro-judgments. *Look what she's feeding her kids,* or *Look what she's wearing,* or *Doesn't that guy know what cigarettes are doing to him?...* stuff like that. Thoughts that, in effect, showed me where I stood in comparison.

That behavior was wrong of me. It was none of my goddamn business.

But judging others is one of the ego's biggest defense mechanisms, and it reflected on me how I viewed myself. Most of us are guilty of it to some degree. But one day, I realized it was a telltale sign of not loving myself...

That One Day

A most wondrous thing happens when your self-love improves: You stop judging yourself so harshly. And when you stop judging yourself, you actually stop judging other people, too. These two things create more bliss and happiness in your life than you might expect. It's *extremely liberating.*

So here's what happened that one day... I was in someone's house and looking at a picture of a couple who'd just been married. I was smiling, because it was a wedding picture, and weddings are happy. But then something dark happened. I started thinking about the weight of the people in the photo.

I'm not proud of that moment, but it did serve as a lesson. I stopped myself in my tracks when I realized how horrible it was for me to be judging their weight. But I know exactly why I was drawn to focus on this. You see, I was judging them... *because I judged myself about **my** weight all the time.* I used to hold *myself* to such a crazy-high standard when it came to fitness and having a trim body that I automatically projected my point of view *of myself* onto other people. Ack!

But the great thing is that, as you start to love yourself more, this need to compare goes away. You cease to judge yourself cruelly on things that don't matter, and as a result, you stop judging other people. When this happens, everything in your life gets better. Seriously better.

This goes both ways, too. You can use this to think about other people *who judge you.* When they're judging you, it's only because it comes from their own insecurities about themselves. It's never really about you. When people judge, they're looking outside of themselves to feel secure, or good, or right, or superior. But when we love ourselves, we don't look outside ourselves for confirmation because we already feel it within.

This doesn't mean we can't seek to improve our lives in all kinds of ways, but now the change will come 100% from a foundation of self-love! So, if you start every morning saying things like, "*I love me just as I am today. I love my body. I love my life,*" you grow a strong foundation of self-love and self-worth, and this makes you less judgy... of you and the people in your world.

Love Thyself Unconditionally

Now that I've taken my self-love to new heights, I do not place conditions on myself in order to love myself. I love myself as I am today, here, now.

Loving yourself doesn't mean you get lazy and stop striving to improve or make better choices. In fact, you try to even more, because you love yourself! It doesn't mean settling for less than your best. It's the opposite. When you love yourself unconditionally, you're more vested in living your best life possible. You want to treat yourself wonderfully, as well as everyone around you. You want to take care of your body, because you deserve it. You're so in love with you, and your life, that you want to live to be 180 years old!

Loving yourself also means being gentle and caring toward yourself through transitions and changes, like menopause or aging. I might want to improve some things about myself, but I do this loving myself through the whole process. Loving myself is why I want to be my best me. Because I'm worth it. And so are you.

What else does this mean for me? I reduced the use of filters on my social media posts. I know there are some playful ones with puppy dog ears, etc. I'm not talking about those. But what does it say to our souls when we constantly show up with a plasticky, smoothed-out, filtered face? You get so used to it that, if you post a photo without it, you'll start to *not* like how you look. Worse, you won't like looking at yourself in the mirror, when your smiling face should be one of the happiest things you see all day. So, to me, these filters are a dangerous place to go. And certainly not one I want to teach my daughter.

I would say I'm embarrassed that I didn't figure all this stuff out at a much younger age. But look at what our culture promotes... a thousand messages a day telling us we're not good enough. I was broken by this for many years. I still occasionally fall for it, but now I'm aware more often than not.

I love myself, and so I treat my body with respect. I eat well most of the time, I use moisturizer to make my skin feel good and soft. I use makeup sometimes (I love glittery lip-gloss!). But I don't let these define me. They're not tied to my self-worth. I don't criticize my body or skin. There's nothing wrong with enhancing yourself if you feel good about doing it. I merely want to suggest that it can be a slippery slope, and the most important thing is self-love, and not feeling like you *have* to be a certain way. That you love yourself just the way you are, in all your radiant glory.

Lipstick Self-Talk

I love my body just the way I am.

My butt is lovely just the way it is.

I am whole and healthy.

I am beautiful inside and out.

I am kind to me. I adore my body.

CHAPTER 14

FUN SELF-LOVE TIP: SELF-LOVE LETTERS

You are worthy of love and affection, and don't you ever forget it. Write yourself love letters, and fall in love with yourself first.

— AMY LEIGH MERCREE

One of my favorite acts of self-love is writing a love letter to myself a couple of times a year. I'm talkin' stationary, nice pen, stickers, and even a kiss with my lipstick smacked right next to my signature at the end. And that's what you're going to do!

Get a piece of paper (it doesn't have to be fancy). Write "Dear (insert your name)," and really make it a love letter, from you to you. And profess your love to yourself. This exercise is beyond powerful, and it's a double-whammy of self-love because you experience self-love when you're writing it, and you experience self-love when you receive it in the mail. That's right, you're actually going to mail it to yourself!

After you write your letter and sign it, put on your lipstick, and give it a nice, big smack of kissy love next to your signature. Then, stick it in an envelope, stamp it, wait a week, and drop it in the mail. You can also ask a friend or family member to stick it in the mail sometime in the next couple of weeks, so you won't know when to expect it. By the time it arrives, you'll likely have forgotten about it, and it'll be extra fun when you receive it!

CHAPTER 15

THE SELF-AWARENESS SUPERPOWER

*A wise woman once said, "F*ck this shit," and she lived happily ever after.*

— QUOTE ON A CANDLE

The Self-Awareness Backbone

"Chirp, chirp," peeps the canary in my coal-mine mind.

I respond: I sniff the energy. I squint my eyes a bit. Yep, I need to change my energy.

When you love yourself, you gain an extra superpower: *self-awareness*. It's one of my favorite parts of the self-love journey, because when you're self-aware, you're ready for any situation that comes along and disrupts your day, jolts you, or yanks your magic carpet out from under you.

Because, if there's the slightest whiff of stinky air, you know it.

You're a bloodhound.

You smell that something's off.

You adjust.

You quickly attend and take corrective action.

How does this happen? Well, your self-awareness superpower is about *being so in tune with your energy shifts,* that you take immediate action. It makes you present. It allows you to course-correct. Self-awareness increases your intuition. Your *situational awareness.* And all of this is fundamental to living your magical life.

This self-awareness superpower helps you pick up on potential issues quickly, where you're like a detective, raising a single brow when something fishy happens. It's the little yellow canary in the coal mine of your mind, bringing things to your attention. *Chirp. Chirp.*

This might seem obvious, but you'd be surprised by how many people ignore all of the little sensations and feelings that happen on any given day. Even more fascinating is how many don't even know these shifts in their energy happen, subtle or big. Heck, some think it's indigestion. I jest. Sorta. The point is that, when you're self-aware, you notice right away, and you handle things right away. There's no waffling, no ignoring. When you feel off, you take action. If your energy feels icky, you pick up on it and take action by doing your Lipstick Self-Talk, having that nice cuppa tea, having a mini-dance party in your office with the door closed, or screaming into your pillow. Or taking action can be something big, something life-changing, like walking out of a job, or a relationship. Or moving to another city. Or country!

The point is, you don't let things spiral out of control, because you detect small changes in your vibe immediately, and take quick, corrective action.

Just Sayin' No

With your self-awareness superpower, it's much easier to say no to things, and people, and events. You even learn to say no to yourself.

When is this a good thing? When you tend toward laziness or giving in to temptations. Or the opposite: When you're an overworking, Type-A person, never stopping to smell the roses, or take some time off. With self-awareness, you comfortably say no to things that are bad for you. Your canary softly chirps, alerting you of a potential problem—*chirp, chirp*—and you do whatever is best for you instead.

Lipstick Self-Talk

I am strong in my beliefs about my choices.

I don't waiver, I don't falter. My energy guides my life.

I am my own hero.

I am dynamic, playful, and fun.

I can shift my vibe on a dime.

Exercise

What are you good at? It can be anything: speed reading, eating your weight in watermelon, playing tennis or billiards, microwaving popcorn, or braiding hair with your toes... for anything you are good at, from small things to big things. Be bold with your list. Write five things here!

_____

_____

_____

_____

_____

CHAPTER 16

STEP TO IT! CHOP CHOP!

Until you value yourself, you won't value your time. Until you value your time, you will not do anything with it.

— M. SCOTT PECK

I usually share life lessons oozing love, and gentleness, and inspiring sparkles. It's my nature. But I also sometimes need to open up a little can of whoopass. Today's a day for that because some of you might be reading this book and still thinking, *Poor me, whoooa is me. How will I ever do this self-love stuff?*

And although I've explained that you simply need to start with the words in your head, I want to add something important:

This is all up to you.

I mean, come on, if you want this bad enough, you *will* show up and do the self-love. You'll implement the principles in this book. You'll do your Lipstick Self-Talk. Every day.

Self-love is a journey. But, as you know, every journey begins with a single step, and nobody can move your sassy ass except for you.

The Tough-Love Trainer

Back in my bodybuilding days, I had a trainer who only wanted people on his team that took it seriously, people who wanted it badly enough. So every week, we were measured to make sure we were progressing toward our goals. And we were allowed to slip up *once*... if one week, your measurements had not improved enough (or had gotten worse), then he might give you more cardio or weight lifting to do, or he might put you in the doghouse. But if you showed up another week in the same situation, with no improvement or getting worse, you got *kicked off the team*. Bam, just like that. He didn't want to waste his time on you. He only wanted people who were serious. He only wanted champions.

I'm not saying you need to be that tough with yourself, but the story is a reminder about the importance of dedication and commitment.

> *If you want something enough,*
> *you must be willing to do the work.*

It's what I do. I don't just write about this stuff, I *do* the stuff. Every damn day. I do the principles in my books like they're a full-time job. I *make* the time to do it. I turn off my phone. I turn off social media. I do my self-talk. I journal. I get enough sleep. I meditate. I exercise and move my body. I love myself. In other words, I show up for my life. Because when I show up, I have the most magical life.

And the same goes for you.

This is up to you.

Your life is not determined by your past. This is not about your parents. Or your partner. Or your friends. Or your coworkers. **This is**

about you. And your love of yourself has to be more powerful than your past programming, circumstances, and experiences.

You might be thinking to yourself, *But my love for myself is **not** more powerful right now.*

Excuse me while I open up my can of whoopass and say, *That's shitty self-talk!*

You must start with your words. It's that simple.

Or you might tell me you don't have time. Or you have eight kids under the age of four. You might be too tired. And you know what? You, of all people, need to get your ass on the self-love train!

Let me find some time for you...

- When you get up in the morning, from the moment you swing your legs off the bed, to the moment you step into the bathroom... say to yourself, *I am worthy I am worthy I am worthy.* There is nothing else going on at this time, so you're free to focus your attention on your words.
- When you're using the toilet, put down your phone, and start thinking and saying positive self-talk to yourself.
- While you're brushing your teeth, look at yourself in the mirror and say, over a mouthful of foaming, minty toothpaste, *Hi, babe, I'm gonna have a sparkle shine day today.* Then smile a toothpasty smile at yourself.
- While you're washing dishes, while you drive your car, while you walk to the mailbox... these are all times for you to focus on your positive self-talk.
- And, of course... while you're putting on your lipstick!

So, please, don't tell me you don't have time. I just found you many little opportunities throughout your day.

But you know what? I'm in a generous mood, and I'm going to find you even more.

Did you know... it's okay *not* to answer a phone call? It's okay *not* to reply to a text or email right away. It's perfectly acceptable to *ignore* social media for an entire day, or week, or month (everyone will still be there when you return). It's *brilliant* to take a day off. It's *lovely* to make easy, one-minute smoothies for dinner for the whole family. It's *super fine* and very much recommended to do *nothing* sometimes. All these things are A-OK! And they're great acts of self-love.

There. More pockets of time for your positive self-talk. You're welcome. :)

Lipstick Self-Talk

I take responsibility for my life, and it starts with self-love.

I am worth taking time in my day for self-love.

I show up to my life, so I'm the best me I can be. I'm in charge!

I see the look in my own eyes, and I know I'm loved and honored.

I am thankful for taking such great care of myself.

CHAPTER 17

THE LOVE BUS—WANNA TAKE A RIDE?

This life is mine alone. So I have stopped asking people for directions to places they've never been.

— GLENNON DOYLE

"What do you want?" Mom yells into the phone. From across the house, it rattles me from my peace. I'm sitting in my Juju Corner, my secluded, cozy little spot in my mom's house, where we lived during COVID lockdown. My Juju Corner is where I go for inspiration and meditation.

"Why are you calling me?" My mom continues screaming.

I swallow.

I put in my earplugs.

I go back to my self-love with a breath. Deeper this time.

Mom continues barking into the phone. *"Stop calling here! Take my name off your goddamned list!"* She hangs up the phone, cusses colorfully to herself, and then walks back into the bedroom to resume her normal conversation with my stepdad. Meanwhile, my ears are singed from the fire, and it wasn't even directed at me. The funny thing is, she's feeling normal now. She's nowhere near as rattled as I am, the outsider.

I understand her frustration. Her name is on every telemarketing list in existence, and random strangers call her phone multiple times a day selling things. She has a lot on her plate, as she cares for her husband, who's gradually losing his mental faculties to dementia. She has three dogs, two of which have health issues and require extra care and patience. And? I love her. I wish so much that she could cultivate more peace in her life, for her own well-being, and for the energy she puts out. But... although I can bring a horse to water... I can't make her drink.

Energy: Everyone Has Their Own

We're not alone. We live with other beings on this planet. So the question is, how do we manage this experience? How do we keep our elevated energy soaring high above the fluffy clouds, where it feels so awesome, when the human experience requires living in a world with people who aren't doing the same?

There are no magic bullets here, but *we're all in charge of our own life and mindset*. Here are some tips:

- Obviously, you'll probably want to minimize encounters with negative people. I wholeheartedly recommend that. If you have cranky people at work, or an angry neighbor, or family you live with who aren't on your magic-carpet-riding life, then minimizing the time together will help. *And let me add with a stern tone*: You're not to feel bad about doing this. It's okay to prioritize that which makes *your* heart sing, not crumple. And if we take responsibility for our own happiness, we can help teach others to do the same.

- But it's not possible to eliminate all soul-challenging encounters. I know. And this is where you amp up your self-love routine. You add extra self-care into your day, especially before and after these encounters. If you're going to visit your in-laws, and it might be a stormy ride for your mind, then jack up your self-love the hour before going. Or heck, the whole day before, and tap into it during the visit—spend time in the bathroom doing Lipstick Self-Talk! And then definitely stoke your self-love fire immediately upon exiting the scene.

- Another incredibly effective solution is *music*. If I'm around someone negative, then the second I have the opportunity, I put on my mood-shifting, soul-lifting tunes. From there, once your mind and heart have had a moment to reset, you can dip into your positive self-talk. Say a few lines, and take some deep breaths. Visualize glittery, rainbow energy all around you. It really works.

- Oh, and smile. A smile always makes your brain happier, even when it's forced. But the bottom line is that we can't let other people's energy dictate ours. This is easy to say, but it can be hard to do. Fortunately, it gets much easier with practice.

Getting People on Your Love Bus

I'm sorry, but not everyone is going to ride your Love Bus. But just as somebody's negative energy can impact you, the flipside is true. Your energy can impact them. I wish it were as easy as clapping my hands or wiggling my nose like Samantha in *Bewitched* and telling the other person to switch their energy to positive.

Unfortunately, this can backfire. In the heat of the moment, acting too positive can make them feel worse, not better, and they'll dig in their heels.

And if you attempt to bring it up at a different time, when they're in a better mood, it's still not very effective. The ego has a way of resisting change, and most people don't like unsolicited advice.

What's the stealthy strategy? The very best advice is simply to be the beaming star you are, and inspire people through *your* actions. There's a growing field of research called *emotional contagion*. It shows that our moods can powerfully impact one another. Happiness and positivity are wonderfully contagious, which is why you'll laugh much harder at a comedian when you're surrounded by other laughing people. Similarly, when you give off good vibes, you influence others positively, in a ripple effect that may ultimately affect many people. Consider the simple act of giving someone a smile, an effortless way to share free happiness and make the world just a little bit better, each time you do it. And that's an incredible power we all hold, so slap a sloppy grin on your face when you're around others, and watch what happens.

People will notice when they see you smiling, floating through life, feeling good and rarely bothered by anything. Most people want that! Most will simply observe from a distance, but some might even ask questions. *How is it that you're always so happy?* You won't be able to influence everybody in your life, but some of them might just hop on board your magical Love Bus. So keep shining!

But Let's Talk About *You*

This is a self-love book *for you*... it's about *your* self-love. The reason I talk about spreading joy to others is because doing so helps improve *your* environment and *your* life experience. We all like being surrounded by other self-loving people. *It's awesome!*

Don't get frustrated when other people don't want to take a ride on your Love Bus. Sometimes they do, and sometimes they don't.

The most important thing is keeping your self-love shining bright for your life.

If you're driving a big ol' Love Bus by yourself, and no one is riding with you, that's just fine. In time, there will be people who come on board. Some who come and go. Some who stay forever. But know this: I'm driving a Love Bus too, and there are tons of others like us out there! As you might imagine, my bus is pink and yellow with glitter, and shimmer and twinkles and bells. Oh, and fuzzy dice! It has infinite seating for others. The windows are always open, and fresh air flows through on the words of loving self-talk.

Lipstick Self-Talk

I love myself so deeply, it radiates out of me and touches others.

My loving energy is healing to me and healing to others.

I love seeing people smile at me, a reflection of my own smile to them.

I love setting a happy example.

I am a magnet for happiness, and I make others happy, too.

CHAPTER 18

BUTTERFLY LIVING

Listen to your heart and intuition. Somehow, they already know who you are to become.

— STEVE JOBS

You're well on your way through this book, and your self-love is growing and growing. As a result, you might realize you have new and different dreams before you. That's because, as your confidence grows, you start to see the world through different eyes. You start to imagine glittering possibilities that shine on the horizon, like the Emerald City in *The Wizard of Oz*.

There are choices.

There are chances.

There are opportunities all around you.

You're transforming into a beautiful new soul who loves yourself, because you know that's how you can best help the world. You're a person who has granted yourself permission to be who you are destined to be. A person who is madly in love with yourself inside and out, and you take responsibility for your own destiny. A splendid person with confidence and boldness, and a person who gets playful when things go wrong. A person who has learned to forgive. This is the new you, a glorious, magnificent butterfly. With rainbow-colored wings, luminous in the sun, flying from flower to flower, goal to goal, dream to dream. You are amazing.

So, my lovely friend, *what are your new dreams?*

Today's lesson is acknowledging the new you that you're transforming into. Celebrating your efforts. This new rockstar you, this new butterfly, this new illuminated person. Take some time to reimagine a new life as the new person you are becoming.

Lipstick Self-Talk

I am transforming. I am epic.

I have new beliefs. I have new dreams.

I evolve and grow. It's who I am. It's who I want to be.

I'm bursting with love for my self. I am exquisite!

I am a happy, happy person.

Exercise

Think of the greatest life you can imagine...

What would you like to do? How would you live? What would a typical day be like? Would your life have epic happiness? Sexiness? Millionaireness? Think about it. So fun! All the things you want, make a list. Imagine everything is within reach. You don't have to know how something will happen, just imagine the end result. Write it all down here.

CHAPTER 19

FUN SELF-LOVE TIP: CREATE A MAGICAL SELF-LOVE SANCTUARY

Creating a home that reflects your personality and passions is an empowering form of self-love.

— KARA ELISE

As you know, because I keep repeating it (hehe), your self-love is important because it's the foundation of manifesting your dreams and living your magical life. When you have self-love, you glitter and shine, and you attract amazing things. When you have self-love, it means you feel worthy, and worthiness means deep inner happiness.

One way you can increase your self-love is to have what I call a *Magical Self-Love Sanctuary*. What does this mean? Well, you can do this in one of two ways. You can create a room, or a place in your home, that you call your Magical Self-Love Sanctuary. It might be a place you make beautiful for hanging out, pondering, meditating, reading, or journaling. A place that inspires love and self-care.

But if you don't have a dedicated space to do this, there are many ways to add little gems of self-love to your office, desk, or other areas to make your environment more wonderful. Think of it like sprinkling golden pixie-dust around your home and office. Heck, even your car!

Think about every place you spend a decent amount of time. Yes, your home and office—but let's be more specific... Your desk. Your nightstand. Your bathroom. Your patio or porch. When you're intentional about your environment, you can shape it to amplify your feelings of love and awe.

As I mentioned earlier, when I'm at my mom's house, I have a corner in one of the rooms for myself. I have two dividers put up to seclude my corner. I have a couple of small tables topped with lamps, and crystals, and books, and rose quartz book ends. I have a checkered vase with pink silk flowers. Candles. My orange-blossom face spritz. I have comfy chairs with pillows and leopard-print blankets. I have a mirror, so I can smile and wink at myself. There's a window with stained glass art hanging on a hook. In this *Juju Corner,* I come up with a lot of book ideas. It's where I journal, where I explore my heart and mind. It's where I tap into my inner juju.

Many factors contribute to the totality of your environment. Your preferences may vary, but I generally feel most uplifted in a spa-like environment. Spas have, through decades of trial and error, perfected environments for making people feel relaxed. Here are some things to consider for making a Magical Self-Love Sanctuary:

- Clutter-free—A cluttered environment clutters the mind and heart. If you have things laying around on tables, like piles of papers, or clothes, or dishes, they act like roadblocks to clear thinking and feeling. Elevated emotions can wither when distractions like this snag your attention. So tidy up. Get organized. This alone will increase your self-love flow and dramatically improve your environment.
- Beauty—Any addition of beauty to your environment is simple self-love. I love salt lamps, candles (LED or real), flowers, crystals, and pretty little LED fairy lights.

- Natural sunlight—Sunlight puts you in a good mood. A 2005 study published in *Psychosomatic Medicine* showed that hospital patients who were exposed to more sunlight required fewer painkillers. If you have a room with a beautiful window, it's a great place for self-love.
- Nature, of any sort—An outdoor setting, fresh air, a gentle breeze, plants, colorful flowers, and trees all contribute to your well-being.
- Water features—Nothing beats the sound of a babbling brook for tapping into your inner calm. Even a small desktop fountain works wonders for the soul. I have one of these in my bedroom, and we sleep with it on all night. There are also apps for simulating this sound.
- Pleasant aromas—Fresh flowers, incense, essential oils. I have peppermint essential oil by my desk, a bottle of lavender on my nightstand, and lemon in the living room. I release a drop from the bottle right onto the floor, or my pillow, or a cushion, when I'm sitting in any of those places. As the drop falls from the bottle to the surface, I smile, knowing it's an act of self-care in that tiny drop.
- Sounds—water (again), wind chimes, birds, music.
- Art—having pictures you love and art that evokes emotions of awe are wonderful for triggering feelings of love.

Make a project for yourself to create your own Magical Self-Love Sanctuary. It's not something to do overnight, nor would you want to. Start with making a list of the things that relax you and bring you pleasure. Then, set a goal to look for these things over the next month or two as you slowly build your own little private sanctuary.

When you're on vacation, it's wonderful to pick up a small memento that you can add to your sanctuary. With different seasons and holidays, you can decorate it differently. I like twinkling Christmas lights in the winter, pink hearts around Valentine's Day, fresh flowers in the spring, and autumn decorations in the fall.

CHAPTER 20

TURNING AN OOOF DAY ON ITS HEAD

Keep watering yourself. You're growing.

— E. RUSSELL

Note: I've discussed *OOOF* days in my book, *The Coffee Self-Talk Daily Reader #1*. If you've already read that, don't worry, keep reading below. I've got more to say about it.

∽

"Shit," I say to myself as I walk into the kitchen. I add in a mumble, "I'm not feeling right. I'm feeling.... like I'm, well, OOOOOOOF. Not my normal sparkly self."

I look at my calendar... *ah.*

Hormones.

I take a breath and shrug my shoulders. Then I say to myself with a bit more love, "Well, at least I recognized it." I pat myself on the back and mentally pivot from what I'd originally planned for my day, because an OOOF day means a day incorporating *more* self-love. OOOF days are special, and they call for a special strategy to help me get my sparkle back.

What exactly is an OOOF day? It's one of those days that slams into you, knocking the air out. Or maybe it's a day that sneaks up on you, lightly touching you with anxiety. It's a day where you can't help but say, "*OOOF!*"

First things first. We all have them, my friend. It's normal. It doesn't mean anything bad about your magical life. It doesn't mean you're doing something wrong. It's perfectly normal to have a day or two, or three (or more!) that rattle your bones. I mean, let's be real... sometimes the self-love journey is two steps forward, one step back. Three steps forward, five steps back. Ten steps forward, a half-step back. But ever forward, that magic carpet flies, with a few detours here and there.

I remember my first OOOF day. I was frustrated and thought I was doing something wrong. Which made my OOOF day even worse! But that was also part of my solution, because I knew something actually must be "off." It wasn't my normal to feel this way. So I dug deep.

I was in northern Italy at the time with my daughter, and my husband was in Bulgaria. He couldn't be with us due to visa restrictions. So there I was, lying on our unmade bed. The fan was blowing on me because it was hot and muggy. Our apartment, like many Italian apartments, didn't have air conditioning. And I didn't feel very happy. In fact, I felt downright anxious. *And I wanted to know why.*

Taking a moment to contemplate my mood, I remembered that I'd felt this way about a month before as well. Huh. Back then, I didn't call it an OOOF day, but I remembered having a day where my sparkle wasn't very bright. I also remembered that the OOOF day *came and went.* That's important.

It dawned on me: Both OOOF days occurred during my cycle. *Maybe it's those wacky hormones!* And suddenly, just knowing the reason behind my slump was enough to relax my clenched soul.

I decided right then that I'd take the rest of the day off and relax. I'd turn this OOOF day on its head. I'd walk to the local coffee bar and have an iced espresso. I would take a book to read and enjoy myself while my hormones did their womanly magic, knowing I'd feel better in a day or two. I discovered that, despite my magic-carpet-ride life, there are still going to be OOOF days. The beauty of self-love is that it helps you navigate these days with more grace.

Surfing the OOOF Day Waters

On an OOOF day, you want to focus completely on what you need in that moment. Right then. Right at the moment you say, *"OOOF,"* you stop what you're doing, and ask yourself, *What do I need right now to feel better?*

It might simply be to sit down. Or maybe take a walk. It might be getting in your car and driving for an hour, windows down, wind blowing through your hair, music blasting. The point is, these days can happen, and you have some tools at your disposal for managing them:

Tool #1: Be Super Gentle With Yourself

This is my biggest advice. Be okay with a choppy-water day. Just let it happen. Let it flow through you. It can be from hormones, a pile of things that finally poked you too hard, lack of sleep for too many nights, low blood-sugar, or anything. The important thing is getting back to your new habits, the new you, as quickly as possible. And you will. So, no worries. I promise. Give yourself a break, and tell yourself that you'll get back on your magic carpet ride tomorrow or the next day.

Tool #2: Walking the OOOF Away

On my OOOF days, the very first thing I do is I go for a walk. It always —and I mean *always*—elevates my mental state. In fact, if I wake up and feel an OOOF day coming on, I go for my walk before I do anything else. The movement stimulates my mind and creativity, it jumpstarts my self-loving heart, and I feel so good that, by the time I get back home, I'm in a completely different mindset.

On the walk, I sometimes listen to music, which is a powerful, *100% effective* tool for changing your state. Sometimes I listen to Coffee Self-Talk scripts I've recorded. Sometimes I say my self-talk, and in this instance, I usually pick one small but *mighty* line of self-talk, saying it over, and over, and over, like a mantra. It always helps me shift my state. My favorite mantra is *I am worthy*. My second favorite is, *I love my life, no matter what.* Those words are powerful. They give me goosebumps just writing them here for you.

Tool #3: Changing Places

Sometimes you can change your state by simply parking your butt in a different location. Such as going into a different room. If you work from home and you're having an OOOF day—don't think this is crazy —but if the weather is good, take a chair out into your garage, open the garage door, pull your car into the driveway, and hang out in the garage. Simply changing your environment can have a profound impact on your energy, whether you're working in the new space, or watching Netflix, or escaping into a delicious romance novel. Sitting in your garage might seem a little extreme, but try this, or something similarly unusual, and your brain can't help but rejigger itself to make sense of its new context. Novelty is the key here, so don't hold back, and don't be afraid to do something a little strange. *Strangeness is the point.*

If you're feeling extra scowly, extra *OOOFY*, then make a bigger change, and go somewhere *totally* different. Get in your car, and drive to a café you've never been to before. Sit your butt somewhere new, look around, and see different things. A change of location changes your perspective.

Tool #4: The Cortisol Angel-Demon

Self-love lowers cortisol levels. Cortisol is the so-called "stress" hormone. When cortisol is coursing through your veins, you feel sucky. Stressed out. But our bodies make cortisol *as a protective mechanism*. Our savannah-dwelling ancestors used cortisol to hide from predators, fight, or run for their lives. Cortisol got their bodies ready to take action!

So in a sense, cortisol can be thought of as an angel, not a demon. But we've got to be smart about it. Otherwise it's a demon. In our cushy, modern times—there's not many saber-toothed tigers in my neighborhood these days—we need to understand that cortisol is dangerous when mismanaged. Because, when you mismanage cortisol, and the stress that causes it, it becomes persistent. And if it keeps coming back, it eventually harms the body. We're designed to use cortisol to handle emergencies, but not for never-ending stress. Chronic stress is very hard on the body, causing inflammation, headaches, lowered immunity, and exacerbating serious illnesses like heart disease. Um, no thanks... say no to daily freakouts or gnawing fears. I won't be able to live till I'm 180 like *that*.

But! If you use cortisol like a red flag waving to get your attention, then it can be your guardian angel. A sort of annoying one, sure. But if you take action when you first notice the feeling of stress, then cortisol can be helpful. It lets you know when you need to make a change. It's there to help save you.

OOOF days usually come with cortisol. It's that shortness of breath or tightness in your chest, your body telling you that you're stressed. And this means it's your opportunity to shift gears toward self-love, self-soothing, and self-care. The good news is that, in time, your self-love leads to decreased stress overall, fewer OOOF days in general! This is because you become so self-aware of the things that cause you stress, that you systematically remove them, one by one, from your life.

The "Clearing My Mind" List

If you feel stressed, the cortisol feeling doesn't have to last. Sometimes, the best thing you can do is simply find something to distract yourself for a little while, so you can clear the cortisol and come back to life feeling more empowered.

The distraction can be anything: watching TV, or reading a book, or like I mentioned, going on a walk, or going to a café and having a steaming cup of green tea while you journal your heart out with a beautiful fountain pen. The goal is to have a list of things you enjoy doing that take about 20 to 60 minutes (see list below). This is usually long enough to chill out and reset. If you feel stressed, tightness, or fear, then grab your "Clearing My Mind" list, pick out an activity, and do it.

When you come back, after your body has processed the cortisol, you'll feel better. It doesn't always mean that whatever poked you before won't poke you again, but now you're in control. And in a much more resourceful frame of mind. You can approach the situation with a clear head.

It's at this time that you can drill down and start asking questions. *Why do I feel this way? What brought this on?* These questions shine the light on things you can change. You'll see that your brain and heart learn, and you get faster and faster at returning to your blissful state each time. Moments of uncertainty and frustration may still come, messy days.... but they don't last.

Before I set you loose on the Lipstick Self-Talk script for OOOF Days, here are some suggestions for your "Clearing My Mind" list:

Buy Someone Coffee—Take the focus off you, and be generous with someone else. Drive through a coffee shop or fast food drive-through, and buy the person's order in the car behind you. Although this is a book dedicated to self-love, sometimes we can come at it from the other side, by helping someone else. Something as simple as purchasing a cup of coffee for a stranger can be a powerful way to lift your spirits.

Plant Herbs—Take a trip to your local nursery, and buy some herbs to plant in your yard or pot in your kitchen. Tending to something like this, giving life to something, is pure magic for your soul.

Humor—Go online and look up a few jokes. I'm serious, read jokes for five minutes. Laughter is incredible medicine.

Step Outside—Being outdoors is great for your well-being. When you're outside, there's nature: trees and grass and birds and bugs. Puffy clouds, sunshine, rain, and breezes or snow. When I walk on an OOOF day, the synergy of being outside in the fresh air, *combined with* the movement of my body, are a reliable way to shift my state back to happiness, reduce tension, and increase my energy and vitality. Exercising outdoors actually has a name: *Green Exercise*, and studies show it leads to positive short and long-term health results beyond what you get from exercising indoors.

Rearrange Your House—Riffing off what I wrote earlier about changing your location to change your mood, you can also just change some aspect of your surroundings. such as rearranging your furniture. Or move your things around in your bedroom, living room, office, or on your desk.

Pet Time—Play with your pet. If you don't have a pet, consider adopting one! Fish, bunny rabbit, cat, or dog, anyone?

Bubble Bath—Take a bubble bath or a hot shower. Put on spa-like music, and slip into relaxation while the warm water soothes your muscles and mind. Even if it's only for five minutes, it's a little dose of loving luxury.

Unplug from Electronics—Sometimes my favorite thing to do is simply unplugging from my devices (phone, laptop, and e-reader). It's calming, and I feel a strange sense of control, which feels empowering. It's great for changing your mindset.

Meditate—Deep breaths, focusing only on your breathing, and letting stillness settle inside you is phenomenal for helping you reset your head. You don't have to figure anything out here or process anything. The simple act of closing your eyes and breathing, listening to your breath, noticing your chest rising and falling, will do wonders for you. The fact that you stop and do this for yourself feels empowering, which is especially helpful when you're stressed from having too many things on your plate. By taking a time out, you take back control.

Sleepy Zzz's—A good sleep can do wonders for your emotions. Whether crashing on your comfy couch for a twenty-minute nap, or going to bed early for an extra hour of nighttime slumber, managing your sleep is a key part of managing your mental state. Sometimes, zonking out to pass the time can be all you need to feel completely restored emotionally.

Call Your BFF—Connect with your best friend via FaceTime or text. Ask how they're doing, and share what's going on with you. For sure, your BFF will pump you up and help put a smile on your face.

Find a New Hobby!—If you don't have a hobby yet, make a list of things you'd like to explore and try out. Maybe it's learning a new language, learning to bowl or play billiards, or French cooking, or calligraphy. (You may have noticed that I'm a fan of fountain pens... I recently discovered these beautiful writing tools, and I discovered that there are all kinds of interesting things to learn about them! Who knew?) You can find classes online for different interests, or locally in your town. Did you know that many community colleges offer non-graded night classes for adults, ranging from *The Golden Age of Pirates*, to mastering Microsoft Excel, to glass blowing, to making electronic music? You can also use Meetup.com to find others in your area who have similar interests (*stargazing, anyone?*). And remember this diamond of a fact: When you set out to learn something new, your brain likes it. You start to feel good right in the moment you brainstorm for things to do, because you're setting goals, which causes your brain to secrete dopamine. Dopamine feels awesome when it's zipping around in your head.

Lunch Date—Meet a friend for lunch. Being in the presence of a friendly face and warm energy is soothing balm for your soul. And when you're with someone who has your back on the days you're not feeling 100%, it feels so good. Turns out, there's science behind these good feelings, too. When we're with people we love and trust, oxytocin buzzes through us, and it feels *realllllly* good.

Game Time—Play a game with a friend or family, or by yourself. It's fun, it's distracting, and it passes the time while you pass away your OOOF day. Board games, cards, video games... it doesn't matter. It's all fun and a good way to reset your frame of mind.

Retail Cheer Session—*Shopping!* So, caveats aside... "retail therapy" is kinda legit. I probably don't have to tell you that spending money can improve your mood and cheer you up, if done strategically. Therapist Peggy Wynne says, "In small, manageable doses, shopping can soothe the soul." It's enjoyable and gives you a sense of control. It can be simple window shopping, or you can take time to hunt for something extra special that requires research and thinking, making it goal-driven, which increases dopamine. You can also bring a friend along and increase your oxytocin while you're at it. All good things.

It probably goes without saying, but retail therapy should be done responsibly, as it can be habit-forming. You don't want to do it too regularly, or become dependent on buying something to make you feel good. I did not turn to shopping to boost my mood when I was in debt, for instance. That would have been financially irresponsible, and it would have only stressed me out more when it came time to pay the credit card bill. But I *did* dabble in little self-nurturing mini-luxuries, like having a cappuccino in a cafe, or getting myself a new pen or journal.

Nature, Again—I mentioned earlier how nature is a powerful stimulator of calm and joy when you're exercising, but you don't have to exercise to experience these benefits. Just stepping out onto your porch and looking at the trees in your yard can spark all kinds of positive activity in your brain. Being outdoors is associated with greater vitality. In Japan, there's a form of therapy called *shinrin-yoku*, which means "forest bathing." It basically means, you go hang out in the forest, and it has been shown to lower stress hormones.

Cool, huh? Now, we don't all live near forests, but even walking down a tree-lined street is great. Don't have a tree-lined street in your neighborhood? Well, my love, get in your car and drive to one, or go to a park. But wait, get this... even if you can't get outside... did you know that you can benefit just from *looking at pictures of nature?* Crazy, right?

A review of studies on the topic by Hyunju Jo, et al, concluded that, "The majority of the studies that used display stimuli, such as photos, 3D images, virtual reality, and videos of natural landscapes, confirmed that viewing natural scenery led to more relaxed body responses."

Wow. Time to change the wallpaper on my computer to a gorgeous nature shot!

Lipstick Self-Talk

I love myself, no matter what, when, where, or why.

I am gentle on myself if I have an OOOF day.

My health is better because I love myself.

Loving myself is the key to everything.

I am relaxed and calm.

CHAPTER 21

THE PLEASURE PRINCIPLE

Because of your smile, you make life more beautiful.

— THICH THAT HANH

Today's lesson is about dedicating ourselves to having more pleasure in life.

To making pleasure a priority.

A *real* priority.

For me, this means...

- Curling up with a book and not feeling one lick of guilt about it.
- It means getting myself a silky soft nightgown and wearing it all day, if I want.
- It means treating myself to little things, whether that's hot buttered toast in the morning, toast with cream cheese in the afternoon, followed by grilled cheese and Aperol Spritz in the evening, while wearing a fluffy, hot-pink boa.

- Or taking a trip to Disneyland to ride roller coasters, perhaps still wearing the pink boa, because those things bring me *tremendous* pleasure.
- It means orgasm. (Yep, that's right.)

On this journey of self-love, when you make pleasure a priority in your life, it boosts your self-worth because *you choose* to make pleasure a priority. You choose to take time to do, give, and receive the things that make you *feel gooood*! And when you fill your mind with good thoughts, and your heart with good feelings—*which pleasure helps you do*—you attract more of these pleasurable things into your life.

Pleasure is a core value of mine because it helps me live my greatest life. It helps me enjoy it. It makes me smile more, which makes even more great things happen in my life. By allowing more pleasure in my life, I discovered more abundance. I discovered a healthier body image. I found more creativity for my work. More peace for my soul.

I discovered so much magic because giving myself pleasure helped me let go and relax.

Having little gems or big diamonds of pleasure in your life—*even every day*—feels healthy and wonderful.

ZOOMING OUT: When we allow ourselves more pleasure, it changes our lives. By choosing pleasure, we are choosing ourselves. And this is the ultimate act of self-love. This self-love builds a powerful foundation upon which everything else gets stacked in your life. I've said it over and over—and I'm going to keep on saying it—if you want to live your greatest, most epic, most amazing life, where things just seem to magically line up, synchronicities are everywhere, opportunities flash around every corner, love is in the air, feeling good is the default... then *you must have a foundation of self-love.*

You get there with your self-talk.

You get there with kindness to yourself.

You get there with befriending your brain.

You get there with pleasure!

Pleasure is for everybody. It's not reserved only for the rich and famous, or people who "work hard." We can all find ways to have more pleasure in our lives. So it's time to make a list of things that bring you pleasure. This way, you always have something ready to tap into. Sometimes we get caught up in living our lives and crossing off to-do items, but taking time to experience true pleasure slips through the cracks.

Well, not anymore.

Here's a fun exercise: Come up with a list of 5 to 10 things that bring you pleasure. For example, I love buttered toast, so I wrote "eat buttered toast" as a source of pleasure for me, and I drew a cute little piece of toast next to it. :) You might put on your list things like watching a movie, drinking a glass of wine, getting a massage, reading a book, going to the beach, or sleeping in. Using the lines at the end of this chapter, write as many things as you can think of that bring you pleasure. And then, come back to your list later, and add more to it. Include teeny things, and huge things, and everything in between. You'll always know that you have access to pleasure with this list.

But wait... I want you to add another thing to your list...

Oh! Oh! Oh!

While we're on the topic of pleasure, let's talk about orgasm, because it's a *very* powerful way to self-love. And seeing as the most important relationship you have is with yourself, that means knowing yourself intimately. Any proper self-love routine includes orgasm, whether you're in a relationship or not. It can be a good ol' romp with your partner, or taking time between the sheets with your own sexy self.

If you don't do this for yourself, or if you're not speaking up enough with your partner, then enough of that. That's a sure sign you're not loving yourself the way you deserve. Get out your megaphone, girl! Playing with your body, taking care of girl business... it's a form of self-healing. Self-empowerment. It's a form of massive self-care, and you deserve it!

Orgasm for Your Best Brain and Body

Orgasm is *sooooo good* for your body and brain. It triggers a blast of feel-good brain chemicals like oxytocin, dopamine (pleasure hormone *extraordinaire*), and endorphins to help with physical pain... no wonder my migraines pause during orgasm. It's also the ultimate de-stressor, like a wrecking ball smashing right through your anxiety. *Empower yourself, girlfriend!* I don't know about you, but after orgasm, I feel like I can conquer the world.

Get Working On It

Self-love and orgasm are a regular part of my magical life. Having a focus on orgasm for pleasure was one of the best things I ever did. It was the ultimate way to put my pleasure first, which did so much for my spirit. The more the better, though it doesn't always have to end in orgasm. Just the mere act of taking time to get to know your body and give it love is equally important.

I love sex therapist Emily Morse's take on how important it is to get to know your own body. She says to take five minutes a day for the next week and simply explore your own body, alone, in private. Take a bath and do it, or pile up blankets on the bed with pillows. Lock the door if you need to. Touch your body, and infuse love and respect into it. Include the insides of your arms and wrists, your feet, your knees, your sternum, and neck. Tickle, pinch, rub, and massage all over, and see what you like best, where, and how. If you have a partner, be sure to share your findings!

Also... buy some beautiful, sexy oil or lube. Use it regularly by yourself, or with your partner. Morse says we're 80% more likely to orgasm with lube, so slather it on with a smile. Again, it doesn't always have to end with orgasm. You might just take a minute here or there of self-care, embracing your body and all the nerve endings designed to feel good. And of course, orgasm can be the end game anytime you desire!

It's time to reconnect with your beautiful, sexy body and feel those illuminating, self-loving feelings.

Lipstick Self-Talk

Pleasure is a guiding principle in my life. I love pleasure.

It feels really good to be alive.

I make pleasure a priority in my life. Oh yes!

My body deserves pleasure.

I am worthy of pleasure. Enjoying my life... is a pleasure.

Exercise

Write as many things as you can think of that bring you pleasure.

....

....

....

....

....

CHAPTER 22

DROPPING THE GUILT

Guilt is not invited to my happiness party—I won't even tell him where it is.

— Affirmators affirmation cards

Today is a day for release. Today is a day to forgive ourselves. Forgiveness from past choices, mistakes, and guilt. Because self-forgiveness is a sparkly stepping stone to living your best life.

Today, we take on a brand-new attitude when it comes to forgiveness. It's time to look forward to forgiving yourself. It's time to make the commitment that you'll always forgive yourself—no matter what. Whether that's a big letting-go, like pushing a car over a cliff, or it's small, like skipping a stone across a lake. It's time to let go and forgive, because true self-love requires *self-forgiveness*.

There is tremendous growth in forgiving ourselves.

I used to feel guilty for having fed my dog a vegan diet, and he ended up with cancer. (I'll never know if the illness was related to his diet, but I certainly wasn't feeding him what dogs are designed to eat.) Then, I carried heavy guilt for feeding my daughter a vegan diet until she was two years old. Despite trying to cover all nutritional bases with elaborate supplements, she woke up one day and couldn't walk right. I feared her nervous system was wrecked from not getting proper nutrients. (I immediately switched to an omnivore diet, and she started walking just fine.) I felt guilty about the debt we carried. I felt guilty for a lot of things, like mistakes I had made with other people... *Ack. I drove myself sick with the guilt.*

But when I started my self-love adventure, I thought back on those black, guilt-ridden days. And do you know what I asked myself? *"What did feeling guilty about any of those things do for me?"* The answer: It made me feel sick. It gave me anxiety, a crappy feeling in the pit of my stomach. It kept me in a cage where I had no room to move.

I realized, feeling guilt didn't help me at all.

In fact, it hurt me.

I mean, sure, I can make better decisions going forward based on what I've learned, but there's no reason to pack the guilt in my suitcase and drag it along on the next journey. So one day, I simply forgave myself.

I said, *"Enough!"*

And tears gushed out of me in relief. I was so grateful to finally release the noose that had been strangling my heart. I cried from the freedom. I cried for the relaxation that sailed through my soul.

> *Owning our story, and loving ourselves through that process, is the bravest thing that we'll ever do.*
>
> — BRENÉ BROWN

The Hawaiian Forgiveness Mantra: Ho'oponopono

Ho'oponopono is a beautiful Hawaiian practice of forgiveness that I learned in a meditation class years ago. It's a soul-healing prayer that helps invoke forgiveness within yourself. Here's how this magic goes... say the following, over and over, anytime you need a little forgiveness hug.

I Love You

I'm Sorry

Please Forgive Me

Thank You

Lipstick Self-Talk

I release, I forgive, and I love.

I am worthy of soul-shifting forgiveness. We all are.

When I forgive, my heart expands with strength, courage, and shooting-star love.

I am so blessed, because I know how to forgive myself.

I appreciate my past. I appreciate my mistakes. I learn. I grow. I move on with ease.

Exercise

Answer the following questions:

1. When you love yourself, how do you talk to yourself?

....

....

2. When you love yourself, what do you wear?

_____

_____

3. When you love yourself, how do you move?

_____

_____

4. When you love yourself, how do you stand?

_____

_____

5. What does a confident you look like?

_____

_____

CHAPTER 23

SASSY SELF-TALK

If you have a skeleton in your closet, take it out and dance with it.

— Carolyn MacKenzie

Today's lesson is about being your most sassy self, and feeling the freedom to embrace your sassy, inner you. So be you, and if that's sassy and silly, and over the top, then this chapter is for you!

I have to say, I'm a passionate, playful, loving, cussing, Italian woman. The funny thing is, my cussing actually comes from love and fun. I rarely cuss out of frustration or anger, but then again, those emotions don't visit me as much anymore.

I want to share a Lipstick Self-Talk script that goes all out, having fun, and being totally sassy and badassy. Sometimes we need that! We need to shake things up. To be over-the-top, energized, and strut our stuff. And we need to do it without worrying what other people might think.

Reese Witherspoon says the best piece of advice she ever received was:

The sooner you figure out that other people's opinions of you are none of your business, and it literally doesn't matter what they think of you, you become free... Totally free.

YES! YES! YES!

Be brave. Be courageous. Be big and bold.

Like I am with my cowgirl boots...

Aspirational Cowgirl Boots

I have a dream to own land someday, maybe with a horse or two. I love imagining myself as a cowgirl in that future. So what do I do to have fun with this goal?

I act "as if"!

I go big!

I wear a baseball hat that has *"COWGIRL"* splashed across the front. Am I cowgirl yet? Nope. But my hat is aspirational! Then, I bought the most amazing pair of cowgirl boots. Not just any cowgirl boots, but boots that shimmer, with sparkling wings stitched on them, and peace symbols in the shape of hearts. These are no ordinary cowgirl boots. They're full-on *sassy* cowgirl boots.

The first time I wore them, I knew they'd make a statement, and I was proud of that. I wanted them to be splashy and sassy, because going all out like that is fun! It's playful. And when we play, it elevates our emotions.

Why Does This Matter?

When we feel high vibes, it helps make our dreams come true faster and easier. If you can be happy while you go after a goal, it makes the goal-getting easier and fun.

As Shawn Achor writes in *The Happiness Advantage*, "Thanks to cutting-edge science, we now know that happiness is the precursor to success, not merely the result."

Let that sink in:

Happiness is the precursor to success, not merely the result.

He goes on to say, "Happiness and optimism actually fuel performance and achievement, giving us the competitive edge that is known as the Happiness Advantage."

There you go... be happy now—don't wait until you reach your goal —and you benefit from a competitive edge in making your badass dreams come true. Research says so!

And that's what my boots do for me. And my hat. And my sassy self-talk. It makes me happy and playful, and as a result, I'm more creative. I make better decisions. I'm healthier. I'm living a more magical life.

So with that, I present to you a Lipstick Self-Talk script that's sassy to boot! ;) (This one is extra-long... I had a lot of sass to share.)

I highly recommend you put on some shimmery, glittery lip gloss while singing these lines to yourself in the mirror to some heart-thumpin' music.

Lipstick Self-Talk

I am focused and fabulous!

I'm living one hell of an awesome life!

I deserve all the love, abundance, and sexy fun I want!

I am glittery as all get out!

I make shit happen!

I'm in charge of my incredible life, 'cuz I'm sassy-badassy!

I'm successful, energetic, and I'm a gettin'-shit-done kind of woman!

I step to the plate and take charge, 'cuz I'm the Boss Babe of my life!

CHAPTER 24

IT'S NOT ME, IT'S YOU

When I loved myself enough, I began leaving whatever wasn't healthy.
This meant people, jobs, my own beliefs and habits–anything that kept me
small. My judgement called it disloyal. Now I see it as self-loving.

— KIM McMILLEN

You know that famous line when someone is getting dumped, and the other person says, "*It's not you, it's me*"? Well, today, we're flipping that on its head. Today we're saying, "*Actually, it's not me... it's you.*"

Twenty years ago, this was a radical lesson for me, and it changed my life. The lesson? *We're all just trying to get by and make it in the world as best we can.* What does this mean? It means that, when somebody does something (or says something), that bothers you or offends you... 99% of the time, *it has nothing to do with you*. Nothing. Nada. Zilch. It's not you, *it's them*.

Sometimes people do things, and we think they're doing it because of us. But it's rarely about us! Even things that are done by people close to us, like family and best friends. This means that *you don't need to feel bad or question yourself* when someone else does something that seems "off" to you. Even when it's directed at you, there's usually something else going on. When people do weird things, it's simply because they're trying to live their life, trying to survive, trying to find peace. Trying to be happy. Sometimes they do things that aren't "good," but it's not because of you. *It's because of them.*

I remember exactly where I was when I first heard this idea. It was twenty years ago, and it hit me like a bolt of lightning, and changed how I viewed what was happening in my life. You see, I had just left my first husband. I was driving across the country in my blue Geo Tracker, hoping to start a new life, when I learned about this idea that I call, *"It's not me, it's you"* on a Tony Robbins CD.

I sat there at a red light, the Arizona sun beating down above me in the blue sky, trying to understand why I had allowed myself to marry that guy in the first place. And it brought me to a place where I questioned my worthiness. But where did I get the idea that I wasn't worthy?

Oh... my dad.

I've mentioned that my dad left our family when I was young, and although I saw him on rare occasions, I saw it as a mark *against me* that he wasn't in my life more. As a kid, when your father doesn't try to see you enough, you don't question your father, you question yourself.

My Dazzling Dawning

That's when the idea on the Tony Robbins CD hit me. Oh my god, my dad's behavior *has nothing to do with me!* It's *about him!*

My heart opened wide with compassion. For him. And for me. I realized it wasn't me that caused his behavior. It wasn't that I was unlovable or unworthy. It was that my dad was just doing the best he could do with the tools he had. With the wiring in his own brain, from his own childhood and life experiences. Yeah, he didn't do a good job in my opinion—it was a shit job, in fact—*but it wasn't because of me.*

Freedom! Such liberation from this realization. I was like a bird let out of a cage that I'd been trapped in for almost twenty years, without even realizing I'd been a prisoner of my own low self-esteem.

Ever since that life-changing moment, I apply this lesson all the time. Big or small. Got a rude taxi driver? Hairdresser being standoffish on one of your visits? These have nothing to do with you. Somebody gives you a weird look in the grocery store? It's not you, it's them. They're just having a hard time working through something that day, or maybe they're unhappy with their whole life.

Or look at your coworkers... sometimes people we're close to can act out negatively toward us, or suddenly be distant and quiet. Don't stand there thinking, *"What did I do wrong? What did I do to offend them?"* No, it's just them dealing with their own problems. They're trying to make the best of life with the tools they have.

And for crying out loud, if you send someone a text message, and it takes them twice as long as usual to respond, don't assume it's something you did! Maybe they're eating or sleeping, or driving, or busy, or meditating, or stuck in a well, or enacting their own self-love, or working through something.

Quick Caveat: Let's say you're living this new, high-lovin' life. And let's say you have a friend who starts to seem distant. And let's say it's actually because they're suddenly not as comfortable with all your self-love and happiness. IT'S STILL NOT YOU. *IT'S THEM!* When you're improving your life, there might be times when others close to you need to adapt to the change. Give them time. And if they don't ever come around, well, it's okay for people to change their roles in each other's lives, or to part ways.

A Funny Thought

I'll conclude with a funny card from the *Affirmators* deck of affirmation cards, which cracks me up, but speaks the truth of today's lesson.

If someone speaks unkindly to me,
I'll remember that they've got something going on
that has nothing to do with me.
Like maybe they just pooped their pants.
Yes, that's probably it.

Lipstick Self-Talk

My worth doesn't change because of other people.

We are all here to learn our own lessons.

I am grateful that I now understand that, when others behave a certain way, it has nothing to do with me.

I am comfy and cozy in my own skin. I let other people do their own thing.

I am on a mission of self-love, and I dance my own dance... jiggy-jiggy-bop.

CHAPTER 25

FUN SELF-LOVE TIP: SHAKE YOUR TA-TA'S

We must have the stubbornness to accept our gladness in the ruthless furnace of this world.

— JACK GILBERT

Today's self-love tip is about shaking your ta-ta's and jiggling your butt. You know... *moving your body!* Throwing your hands up. Dancing a jig.

Bottom line—you've got to *move*. Movement creates fresh and flowing energy. And when this happens, old, stagnant energy gets pumped out of the way. Anxiety and confusion blow out. Clarity flies in. It's like opening the windows to your soul and letting life's airy breeze fly through your life. Invigorating you!

When you move, your energy moves, and it improves.

After sitting for an hour, moving your body feels better from the first little step you take. Movement creates ideas. Movement is a way to nurture your body and your soul. So I will scream from the rooftops:

Get up and shake your ta-ta's. Set your alarm and get up every waking hour. You can dance, you can walk, you can do cartwheels. Whatever you do, you move.

And?

I love you.

CHAPTER 26

SELF-LOVE WHEN MAKING MISTAKES

Be gentle with yourself, learn to love yourself, to forgive yourself, for only as we have the right attitude toward ourselves can we have the right attitude toward others.

— WILFRED PETERSON

Last year, I made a tiny blunder on social media, a situation I could've handled better. It caused my mood to dip slightly that day, but the good news was that my reaction was vastly different from how it would've been years before. That's because, as your self-love grows, you respond better to stressful situations. Your heart doesn't race as fast, and your stomach doesn't drop as far.

One reason for this is simply because of self-love.

When you love yourself, you're gentle on yourself.

But there are other reasons...

You see, things that upset you have usually *already* happened. And anything that has already happened is, by definition, in the past.

One of the most powerful lessons for relaxing my racing heart in times like this, even if I'm fresh off a gnarly stress ride, is realizing *it's in the past*. Like, literally, in the past. And there's nothing I can do to go back and change it. But what I *can* do is move forward. I can love and learn. I can pluck from it the gems of wisdom for the future, even if it's, "Well, I'll never do *that* again," and move on.

You learn a lesson.

And if you made a *big* mistake, then you learned a *big* lesson.

Resilience Is Sexy

Rapid recovery is the name of the game here. We all make mistakes, but we don't all handle them well. The goal is to be *resilient*. To bounce back. And resilience is sexy. When you stand up, dust yourself off, and take the next step—*that's resilience*. And you'll become more resilient with more self-love. When you love yourself, you're more courageous. You're not afraid to fail, because your self-worth isn't tied to always succeeding. Which means you eagerly take more risks, and the ones that pay off launch you in bold new directions.

Your self-love makes you braver, no matter how gusty the wind blows. Taking more chances can mean more fails, but this is great because it's where the real juice resides, the *marrow of life*. You're learning valuable lessons, harvesting diamonds, rubies, and sapphires from your experiences. As you learn, you improve and grow. It's your self-love that helps you cope with any failure, and there's no embarrassment or shame when you make a mistake. If you make a mistake that affects someone else, you apologize and move on, without feeling the need to beat yourself up. Why? Because you love yourself, and you don't beat up on things you love.

Life is always moving forward. I love myself through failures and mistakes, because people grow more through challenges than during easy-peasy times. It's times like this that I step into the bathroom, close the door, and look at my eyes in the mirror. I give myself a nice little pep talk. I say to myself, out loud, *"I'm okay. Good for me, for recognizing this mistake and loving myself through it."* And then I give myself a little smile and a nod.

That might seem weird. But if you can tell yourself that you love yourself, even when you make mistakes, then your self-love will glow and grow. This gets you back to living your magical life.

Family Lessons

When I make a mistake, I sit down and talk to my daughter about it. I tell her what I did and how it made me feel. I also tell her how my happiness was not based on avoiding mistakes, and that mistakes are okay. That failures are learning opportunities, teaching us how to make better choices in the future. This allows her to see me as human, and she gets to see how I love myself through challenges and failures. And then she gets to learn from my mistakes. She gets lessons for living her own life.

Playful Living

One of the best things you can do is train yourself to laugh at your mistakes and fails.

Years ago, when my daughter was born, I read a book called *Playful Parenting* by Lawrence Cohen, which teaches techniques for teaching children without resorting to fear and threats. Now for the twist... I apply its lessons to *my* grown-up life!

By forcing myself to chuckle when I make a mistake, it lightens the mood. It eases my tense stomach a bit. Once you've done this a few times, it becomes your default to chuckle when something goes wrong. Try it. We've all experienced incidents that seemed bad at the time, but we laugh at now. So remember that. Just knowing that laughter will come is enough to lighten the mood.

Lipstick Self-Talk

I forgive myself when I make mistakes.

I am kind. I am kind. I am kind.

Today is my day!

I love learning and growing. It makes my life interesting.

I laugh at myself and every mistake I might make. I love me!

Exercise

Answer the following questions:

What are some mistakes you've made, and what did you learn?

_____

_____

_____

_____

What is a mistake you've witnessed someone else make that taught you, such that you were able to avoid making the mistake yourself?

_____

_____

_____

_____

What lesson from a mistake would you pass on to others?

....

....

....

....

CHAPTER 27

BREAKING THE CHAIN

When things change inside you, things change around you.

— Unknown

My earlier life had a lot of starless nights. My first marriage was a mess. Because I had low self-worth, I married the wrong person for the wrong reasons. Oddly enough, at the time, I didn't think my self-esteem was low. I saw myself as a go-getter. Confident. Disciplined, organized, and fit. I had a solid work history and good grades in college. But when my mom met my fiancé, she saw nothing but red flags, and she warned me. The fact that I went ahead and married him anyway speaks volumes about my mental health back then.

So where did that low self-esteem come from?

Why was it so easy for me to fall into unhealthy relationships? To be honest, part of it probably came from watching my mom, a beautiful and talented woman, who didn't know her own worth either. She could counsel me on my choices with the sage wisdom of a sassy monk, but applying it to herself was another story. *Don't do as I do, do as I say.*

That said, times are different now. We know some things about the brain that we didn't know when Mom was raising me, and they definitely did not know when my grandparents were raising my parents. I appreciate this, and I feel compassion for my parents. But that doesn't mean that I don't break the chain with the new knowledge I possess.

The Light In the Dark Past

Do I walk through life focused on my past, ruminating on my "unfair" struggles, or the bad choices I made from faulty wiring and not loving myself enough? Sure, I could choose to do that. But it won't bring me radiance or happiness. That life would suck. In fact, it *did* suck. I lived it.

Until I didn't.

I woke up one day and changed my routine, I changed my habits, I changed the words in my mind so that I'd stop reinforcing the old me, and I could break out and become the new me. And here's how I see it now: My past served to get me where I am today. Very simply.

And when I look at it this way, I can step beyond it. Because here's the sobering truth:

We get rainbows from storms.

We understand light from experiencing darkness.

We know beauty from witnessing the grisly.

Ralph Waldo Emerson said, "*The woods are dignified by comparing them to cities.*"

Know that your new magical life you're living is that much more magnificent and bright *because of your past*. Appreciate the light from the dark. Give thanks to your past, and have gratitude that it no longer rules you. You rule *it*.

Lipstick Self-Talk

My life flows, and I go with it.

I'm kind. I'm love. I'm fabulous.

I feel great because I take care of myself.

It's time for new experiences.

I approve of myself. I love myself. Everything works out well for me.

CHAPTER 28

THE EATING GRAPES ACHIEVER

And now that you don't have to be perfect, you can be good.

— JOHN STEINBECK

I used to be a perfectionist. I was an over-achiever, and I wore my hardass willpower like a badge of honor. I had a Type-A personality with a mindset of *go-go-go*. I felt guilty for taking breaks or resting. I was strong in my will to push-push-push, and I tore through my life and my work like the Incredible Hulk.

Truth be told, I was using busyness to cover up and ignore my own needs. Never mind that I lived a rushed, frenzied life, like tidal waves were always crashing through me. One, after another, after another, and feeling like I was gasping for air with each hit. And never mind that I was impatient with others not stretching to their limits on a daily basis like me... *How dare they?* After all, I was getting shit done, all day, every day. *Why wasn't everybody else? Slackers!*

I had no idea at the time, but my crazy overdrive mentality had been wired in my brain from my own firing and wiring: I operated out of survival mode. Fear. That's how I became that overzealous lunatic, by being afraid that I would miss out on something. The crazy thing is that I thought all of this was good. I was "successful." Right?

Or was I? Perhaps I was successful at meeting deadlines, but I was unsuccessful at other important things in life. Like caring for myself and my well-being.

The truth is, when I lived in crazy survival mode, I never felt magical in my soul, no matter how much money I made. No one would. And I certainly didn't feel legendary. I just felt *tiredly accomplished*. And the drive to continue pushing hard was fueled by fear and by my ego. Because my ego loved when I lived like this. It loved when I tackled things aggressively like a linebacker.

But I discovered a secret that no one had told me about. I discovered that self-love actually *boosts* my efficiency. That self-love would actually lead to *increased* productivity. And that perfection is a lousy goal.

What?

Yeah. Turns out that, when you're not running around like a whacked-out hyena, you actually get more done because you're more relaxed, and this makes you more creative and less prone to make errors. And more likable, too. :)

It's the strangest thing. When I kicked my feet up, like Cleopatra being fanned and fed grapes, my days suddenly flowed more easily. As though the resistance of life was magically diminished. Everything felt so much better.

But don't let me fool you. This new mindset did not happen overnight. On some days, I kicked, and screamed, and doubted. But eventually, I learned that the ideal of perfection is static. Motionless. And impossible, because everything is always changing. So instead, I figured I would just chill out and let life flow the way it's going to flow. And eat some grapes. And that's exactly what I did.

And I discovered the idea that:

Doing something good enough and done...
is better than perfect and not done.

It's like Voltaire said,

Perfect is the enemy of good.

When I started on this self-love journey, my perfectionist tendencies and my Type-A personality clawed at me from the inside. But when I learned that the need to be perfect comes from a place of fear, and that fear is a survival emotion, I saw everything with new eyes. When I learned that living from survival feelings would *not* help me manifest my *Happy Sexy Millionaire* life, I threw my perfectionist, Type-A tendencies out with the trash.

Awesome thing... it ended up being easier than I thought it would be. When perfection ceased to be the goal, work, projects, and my whole life became easier and more fun. Because my worth was no longer tied to being perfect.

Once again, self-love is at the core of making everything go well in life. Love yourself, and you let go of the fear of failing, you become more relaxed, you do more things, you do them better, and everything just magically improves.

Lipstick Self-Talk

I am enough.

I focus on what excites me.

Anything is possible because I love myself.

I am in the right place, at the right time, doing the right thing.

I am a magnet for prosperity.

CHAPTER 29

FUN SELF-LOVE TIP: MIRROR SELF-LOVE MONTH

You don't have to be perfect to be amazing.

— UNKNOWN

When the next month begins, take a dry-erase marker, and draw a big calendar for the current month right on your bathroom mirror. And every day, show up and tell yourself, *"I love you!"*

Draw a heart for the day to mark that you did it. This is a simple, important exercise. It's even better if you share your bathroom with others. My daughter was so excited that she joined me, because... um... *markers and a mirror!*

CHAPTER 30

ROMANCE

How you love yourself is how you teach others to love you.

— Rupi Kaur

The quality of your love life will be 100% influenced by your own self-love.

You must understand that it will be very difficult for someone else to love you fully... until you love yourself. Even if he or she is a wonderful person, and loves you deeply, if you don't love yourself fully, then your partner won't be loving you, they will be loving a shadow of you. An unrealized version of you.

And if you don't love yourself, then you're at higher risk of entering unhealthy relationships, or staying in them too long, or finding yourself bouncing around from one bad relationship to the next. Nothing lasting. Nothing meaningful.

I know, because I was there. I eventually found my soul mate, but only after I went through a lot of dress rehearsals, some of them gut-wrenching. But trust me, the right person IS out there for you... but it will be hard for him or her to find you if you're not shining bright like a star.

"Kristen, You're Not That Special"

I remember lamenting to my mom one day in my late twenties. We were driving along highway 101 in Arizona, the cloudless blue sky expanding over us like infinity. I was whining about how I'd never find a man who could *love like me*. I didn't think men understood big, grandiose love. I wanted someone who didn't play games, who had the same values, who loved to display affection, who wasn't afraid to share his feelings, and who was romantic like the men in the romance novels I read.

She looked at me, shaking her head like I was so naive. She said, *"Kristen, you're not that special."*

Gah! *"What?"*

"Honey, what I mean is... you're not so special that there's only one of you out there. You're not so unique that you're the only one in the world who knows how to love that hard. He's out there."

I looked out the window. I might've blinked. And then I smiled. *She's right*, I thought. How could I be the only person on the planet that's capable of loving as strongly as I did? I would find him. Or he'd find me, or whatever, but he was out there, somewhere. And he was. It's my husband, Greg.

So be patient, and keep building your self-love, so you can find the mate of your dreams.

He's Just Not That Into You

I recently received an email from a *Coffee Self-Talk* reader. She was clearly struggling massively with her self-love, but she didn't seem to know it. She told me how she was so hurt because a guy dumped her... for someone else! But just when she was starting to get over him, he'd call her, out of the blue, and hurt her more by hinting about them getting back together, but then he'd back away again, and this whole cycle would repeat.

I cocked my head at my laptop screen. *HELLO, girl! He's just not into you!*

I almost threw my laptop across the room. *Why in the world would you be hurt over someone behaving like this?"* I was furious. I wanted to reach through the screen and grab her shoulders and shake the hell out of her.

Now, it's not like I've never been dumped or had my heart broken. I had some doozy breakups in my early days. But after reading Greg Behr's book, *He's Just Not That Into You,* some twenty years ago, it was like grenades exploded in my pupils, and I never saw romantic relationships the same. I realized, with lightning speed, how some of the guys I'd dated were *simply not into me!* What a concept! It was like getting snapped with a thousand rubber bands.

To this day, I remember Behr's examples of what to expect if someone is *actually into you,* things like being quick to ask for the next date, being open about their feelings, and really listening to what you say, and your preferences, and then mentioning them later. Upon reading this, my heart had swum in sweet anticipation, in dazzling excitement, *because I'd learned what to look for.* I knew what it would look like to have someone *into* me. Case in point: When I met the man who is now my husband, halfway into our first date, he told me he was having a great time, and asked if I'd like to go out again. Wow! No games, no wondering, *Will he call?* Just total enthusiasm, candor, and *taking action.* And having gotten that out of the way, it made the rest of our first date so relaxed and fun. On our second date, he asked me to be exclusive... *and we've been together ever since.*

To encapsulate Greg Behr's book, here's the bottom line:

When someone is into you, *it's obvious.*
If it's not obvious... *they're just not that into you!*

But how do you attract that kind of interest?

Knowing what to look for is only part of the solution. I still had to do my part, which is—can you guess?— *to love myself.* Only then I could attract that kind of love. And I tell you, when you love yourself fully, *people notice.* You develop a kind of charisma. It's very attractive. When you love yourself, people want to be around you!

So, yeah, I can hurl all the laptops I want when women write to me about the duds in their lives, but at some point, the women have to take responsibility for their part in the play. That means acknowledging that 1) he's not into you, 2) he's doing you a favor, because you're not meant to be together, and 3) when you have deep self-love and self-worth, you won't ever again allow yourself to be strung along by someone who's just not that into you. (To be fair, the guys might not all be duds... they're just not a match for you if your spirits don't connect and catch fire.)

If you're in a relationship, and it's not *ride-off-into-the-sunset* romantic, then take a close look at it. Take a look at you. Did you come to the relationship when you weren't whole and loving yourself first? Or, have you been dumped, and you're still pining away for someone you were *not* meant to be with? Or are you in a relationship that goes back and forth—breaking up and getting back together? That is NOT soulmate material.

True love, the epic stuff they write books about, *is* possible. Games need not be played. You shouldn't be wondering if he'll text or call. You should know where you stand very soon, and after that, always. But if you don't love yourself fully, first, you run the risk of settling for second best, or worse. That's not magical living.

Here's a great little quote for anyone who is single right now, or about to be...

Being single is the perfect place to be found by the right person. Being single is the beginning, not the end.

— R.H. Sin

Lipstick Self-Talk

I matter.

I am important.

My heart is valued, because I value myself.

I am worthy of cinematic, romantic love.

I come from greatness. I attract greatness. I am greatness!

CHAPTER 31

ASKING FOR HELP LIKE A BOSS

You are enough. A thousand times enough.

— UNKNOWN

When I was new to motherhood, I had times when I felt I wanted to run away. Run away from it all, just for a day (or five) and go to some hotel on a lonesome highway. I didn't even care if it was seedy. I just wanted to lie on the bed and stare at the water-stained ceiling. I wanted a break from talking, and doing, and seeing, and hearing. A break from the claws gripping at me.

That was my intuition screaming to me: *Please pay attention. You need to take a break.*

But with my go-getter personality at the time, if you wanted something done right, you did it yourself. So I just kept going and doing everything by myself. Never taking a break, never asking for help.

Well, one day, a scene from the movie, *The First Wives Club,* flashed in my mind. Diane Keaton is telling her friends about the things she does for her husband, and she says something like, "I washed his shorts, I ironed them, and I starched them." Her friends look at her like she's crazy to be doing chores like that! *"You did?"* they exclaim. She replies, *"Well, I supervised!"*

This scene inspired me to make a change. To start asking for help.

And so, in my stressed out, sleep-deprived, new-mommy life, I started to "manage" my household better. I decided it was time to get some help. And I asked Greg to empty the kitchen trash going forward. I know... *haha...* it doesn't seem like a very big ask now, but the idea had never crossed my mind. I had never asked him to do it because I thought of the kitchen as my domain, and therefore my responsibility. After all, the trash can was always overflowing from *my* work in there. I should be the one to empty it, right?

And do you know what he said?

"Sure."

Bam. Just like that, I never had to empty the trash again. He was happy to do it.

Then I asked him to start making the bed in the morning. I was actually nervous to ask him. But it turns out, he'd been wanting to help, but I'd always insisted on doing everything myself. As we discussed it, I came to learn that he actually enjoys doing household tasks, because he works from home and looks for reasons to get up from his desk and move around. He was even happy to *hand-wash* the dinner dishes (I know, right?)... he'd just put an audiobook on his earbuds and go to town!

The more I asked him to help, the more comfortable I became with asking. There was even the time I asked him to do the grocery shopping. OMG—that was huge for me, because, well, let's just say I'm quite particular when it comes to picking out my cucumbers and pineapples. But when my daughter was a baby, I was barely making it through the day, and I finally threw my hands up and asked him to go.

And guess what?

The cucumbers were fine.

Ever since then, I've become a master at asking for help. Whether it's from a friend, family, or even a stranger. Nowadays, for instance, it's not unusual for my husband and daughter to make their own dinners. And not only do they not mind, but the other day, my husband taught my daughter how to make *Nachos Gregorio*. They had a great time!

ZOOM IN: Why is it important to get good at asking for help? Because when you're tired or overburdened, your light doesn't shine, my dear. This drains your energy and your vibe. And one easy way to recharge your batteries is simply by asking for help.

Oh! And here's the best part: When you ask others to help, you empower them. You validate them, demonstrating that you trust their abilities. This is great for any relationship!

Lipstick Self-Talk

I love asking for help.

I pay attention to my mind and my body, so I know when to ask for help.

I love letting people help me, and it makes my life easier.

My heart leads the way with the choices I make.

I easily ask for assistance, like a boss.

Exercise

List all the ways you could ask for help, whether it's doing things around the house, your yard, running errands, at work, or wherever. Get specific... doing dishes, making the bed, laundry, sweeping, cooking, walking the dog, mowing the lawn, braiding your hair, washing the car, carrying in the groceries.

And don't forget where you work. Is there something somebody could teach you that would make your job easier?

Come up with of a bunch of things. Who are the different people you can ask for help? Now go and practice. Pick one of the items on your list, and actually ask for help doing it!

CHAPTER 32
GRIEVING

Love yourself as if your life depends on it, because it does.

— ANITA MOORJANI

My father died last year, and my beloved dog Zeus died about eight years ago. I've also lost two friends to suicide. My nana, with whom I was very close, passed away when I was a teenager. And after an uphill journey with fertility difficulties, I miscarried my first pregnancy. Each of these was a different experience with grief for me.

Death comes in different shapes. It's not just the end of a physical body. For example, I've been through a divorce, and that included grieving. I harbored deep regrets for mistakes I'd made in my life, and I grieved. And I grieved for many years from feeling a lost childhood, burdened by the difficulties of being raised by a single mom in a stressful household.

A few years ago, I went through another mourning process when I realized how badly I had treated myself for so long, and not loving myself the way I deserved. Though the death of that person, the old me, was actually quite welcome. It allowed me to become the person I am today.

Grieving over the "death" of your former self can take on many forms. Some people lose a lot of weight during the process. Moving to a new city or changing careers are other examples of death of the old self. While these may be less severe forms of grief, or based on something that is generally good news, any loss of something familiar—such as habits, a way of life, or moving away from your circle of friends—can make a person sad.

The point is that grief can be caused by different things. But no matter the cause, during such times, self-love is the key for mental health and well-being. Self-love is what holds your hand through it all. It's the glue that holds you together, even when you feel like you're falling apart.

Gentleness

When it comes to grief, and how to manage it, my first thought is about soothing gentleness. When grieving, it's important to be kind and compassionate with yourself and focus on your self-love. This means allowing your grief to take the form it wants to take. Be gentle with yourself as it happens. Let the feelings gush out of you, whether it's intermittent ripples, or a tsunami that hits all at once. Calm or screaming. Or both. It's okay to get it all out. And take peace knowing that everyone grieves in different ways. One of the most important acts of self-love will be allowing yourself to grieve in the way that works best for you.

Most of all, understand that grief is a process, and it's temporary. It will pass. Sadness over the loss of a loved one may never go away, but the debilitating gut-punch feeling is temporary. Grief is a specific emotion, and it has a half-life. It might be days or years, depending on the loss, but on average, every day that passes gets a little better.

Just knowing that the feeling isn't permanent can make it easier to ride out the wave.

Guilt and Grief

For some people, it may seem wrong to be living a magical life when experiencing the loss of a loved one. The guilt can feel like handcuffs. I know someone who lost family, tragically, and he never felt like he completely recovered. But then he started doing *Coffee Self-Talk,* and he began to feel amazing, better than he had in a long time. He had more energy and felt lighter. The clouds were lifting. He started working out and walking through his life with his head up, face tilted toward to the sun.

But then, after a few weeks, his spirit crashed, and he hit a wall. He felt *worse* than before.

His guilt was keeping him from moving on.

Sometimes people can feel guilty for living a beautiful life in times of grief, even years later. But you must remember, when a loved one passes, they wouldn't want you to live on in misery. Just like you wouldn't want your loved ones suffering if the situation were reversed. If you feel guilty for feeling joy, please continue to love yourself, and know that you are worthy of happiness and joy. *They would want that for you.*

When you feel joy in these times, you can think about how some of that incredible energy is *coming from them,* and swirling inside you. They live on through you now, so show them a beautiful time.

Journaling Memories

If someone close to you dies, consider buying a dedicated journal, and start writing down the memories you have of the person. The memories can involve you or not. They can be about the person's big life events or little, everyday elements that spark inside you.

You might find, in this process, that you cry less. Not to suggest that crying not be part of the grieving process; indeed, it can be cathartic and soothing. But you don't have to cry all the time. And this fascinating exercise of journaling life memories can help with that.

Journaling keeps the person's memory alive in you, and it celebrates their life. You create their legacy, through your eyes, and it helps you pass the time as you heal. This legacy aspect taps on something primal in our brains, instinctual, and it soothes. It's also an incredible project to share with other people. Other family members perhaps, or friends. Imagine finishing the journal and passing it around at a dinner gathering of the person's close friends and family. As you pass the journal around, people can read from it and talk about their own memories. Or, of course, you can also just keep it close to your heart.

In the end, no matter why you might grieve, you are never alone. Take any night and step outside to look up into the black, starry sky. We are all made from stardust. We are all here for you, and none of us is every really gone.

Lipstick Self-Talk

I am in harmony with the universe, and I love myself.

I let what wants to come, come, and I let what wants to go, go.

I am calm right now. I have peace right now.

My heart opens to the new loving thoughts in my mind.

I am filled with incredible experiences and memories.

Exercise

Take this space to record a memory of someone in your life who has died (a friend, family member, or a pet). Write about your memories with him or her.

AFTERWORD & FREE STUFF

Every time someone loves themselves better, builds their self-awareness,
understands their patterns, improves their ability to communicate, and
expands their compassion for others, the future of humanity grows
brighter. Your healing impacts the world by bringing in new peace.

— YUNG PUEBLO

Well, my lovely, you did it!

Self-love is here, and you're taking it in. Your soul is growing new wings to fly, and you're making a difference in the world by loving yourself first. Thank you for going on this journey with me. I sure loved sharing it with you.

Now you have more tools to live your most magical life. You have all kinds of great ways to amp up your self-love, because you're a worthy babe! You know the power of growth, learning, and whipping stress into submission, so that you enjoy your life much more.

And now you have your *freedom beat...* your own special groove to move your feet and stir your soul. The one that prompts you to take action, dance to your own music, and sprinkle pixie dust everywhere you go. To be your most powerful you—*your authentic self*—and to make sure you're doing things every day to bring more *pleasure* into your wonderful, magical life!

I love you.

I believe in you.

Now, go live your magical life!

Free Stuff!

Shoot me an email to receive a free gift, the *Lipstick Self-Talk Goodies:* A recorded MP3 file of Lipstick Self-Talk scripts, and a printable PDF of the scripts in this book that you can cut out and tape to your bathroom mirror!

Email me at:

Kristen@KristenHelmstetter.com

Please specify that you'd like the *"Lipstick Self-Talk Goodies."*

A Request

I have a favor to ask of you. Would you please write a review for this book on Amazon? Reviews really help me get the word out. Thank you in advance for taking a minute to do so!

Podcast

You can hear me every week on the *Coffee Self-Talk with Kristen Helmstetter* podcast at the following link or wherever you listen to podcasts:

https://anchor.fm/kristen-helmstetter

And come join our fun and lively group for readers:

Facebook.com/groups/coffeeselftalk

~

What's Next?

Here are the other books in the Coffee Self-Talk family:

The Lipstick Self-Talk Two-Minute Guided Journal:
Little Daily Love Notes to Yourself

The companion journal to *Lipstick Self-Talk.* Build your self-love even faster with this daily, two-minute love-note adventure. Filled with hundreds of daily self-love prompts, like little love notes to yourself. It takes only two minutes a day, but the effects last forever.

The Coffee Self-Talk Starter Pages:
A Quick Daily Workbook to Jumpstart Your Coffee Self-Talk

It has never been easier to dive right into Coffee Self-Talk. This *Starter Pages* workbook takes you by the hand and makes it effortless to get started, with 21 fun, uplifting days of inspiration, affirmations, and simple, fill-in-the-blank exercises to jumpstart your daily Coffee Self-Talk ritual.

The Coffee Self-Talk Daily Reader #1:
Bite-Sized Nuggets of Magic to Add to Your Morning Ritual

This companion book offers short, daily reads for tips and inspiration. It does not replace your daily Coffee Self-Talk routine. Rather, it's meant to be used each day *after* you do your Coffee Self-Talk.

If you do one reading per day, it will take 30 days to complete.

KRISTEN HELMSTETTER

COFFEE SELF-TALK™

GUIDED JOURNAL

Writing Prompts &
Inspiration for Living
Your Magical Life

The Coffee Self-Talk Guided Journal:
Writing Prompts & Inspiration for Living Your Magical Life

This guided journal keeps you *lit up and glowing* as you go deeper into your magical Coffee Self-Talk journey. Experience the joy of journaling, mixed with fun, thought-provoking exercises, and discover hidden gems about yourself. Get inspired, slash your anxiety, and unleash your amazing, badass self.

International Bestseller – Over 150,000 Copies Sold
Coffee Self-Talk: 5 Minutes a Day to Start Living Your Magical Life

Coffee Self-Talk is a powerful, life-changing routine that takes only 5 minutes a day. What if you could wake up every morning feeling more incredible than ever before... in 5 minutes? **Living the most epic life. Your mind mastered!** Coffee Self-Talk transforms your life by boosting your self-esteem, filling you with happiness, and helping you attract the magical life you dream of living. *All this, with your next cup of coffee.*

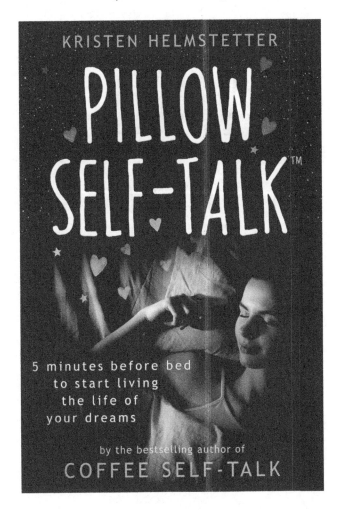

Pillow Self-Talk:
5 Minutes Before Bed to Start Living the Life of Your Dreams

End your day with a powerful nighttime ritual to help you manifest your dreams, reach your goals, find peace, relaxation, and happiness... all while getting the *best sleep ever!*

Wine Self-Talk:
15 Minutes to Relax & Tap Into Your Inner Genius

There is an unlimited source of creativity in you. *Wine Self-Talk* is a simple, delicious ritual to help you relax, unwind, and tap into this inner genius. When you do, watch as your life becomes easier, more exciting, and more fun!

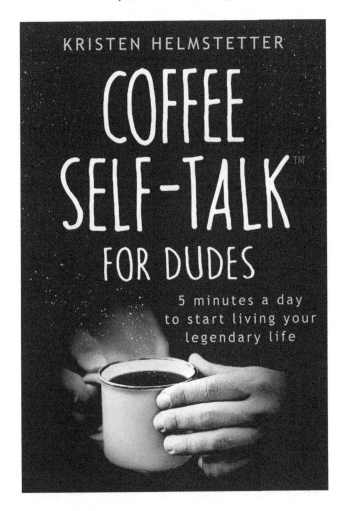

Coffee Self-Talk for Dudes:
5 Minutes a Day to Start Living Your Legendary Life

This is a special edition of *Coffee Self-Talk* that has been edited to be more oriented toward men in the language, examples, and scripts. It is 95% identical to the original *Coffee Self-Talk* book.

Coffee Self-Talk for Teen Girls:
5 Minutes a Day for Confidence, Achievement & Lifelong Happiness

This is written for girls in high school (ages 13 to 17 years old). It covers the same ideas as *Coffee Self-Talk*, and applies them to the issues that teen girls face, such as school, grades, sports, peer pressure, social media, social anxiety, beauty/body issues, and dating.

24580611R00108